WHO'S WHO IN THE BOOK OF MORMON

WHO'S WHO IN THE

BOOK OF MORMON

Robert J. Matthews

Contents

PREFACE

The object of this volume is to present precise analytical biographies of each of the persons mentioned in the Book of Mormon. This seemed a useful project to enable readers to quickly observe the information available about each character. Little attempt is made at interpretation of data, but an effort is made to present the material about each person in the sequence in which it is given in the Book of Mormon record.

An advantage of the biography-type arrangement is that a reader can quickly discern the important points of information relating to an individual, plus the approximate time when the individual lived and something about his relationship to other persons. Thus, this volume serves a much different purpose than a concordance. It would be an impossible task to assemble this material from a concordance, since in order to do so, one would have to know each item beforehand in order to look for it.

Ordinarily, biographies begin with the name of the person; however, the Book of Mormon reports the doings of many persons for whom it gives no name. Part I of the volume presents biographies of those whose names are known, and Part II deals with those whose names are not known, but who are nevertheless significant to the Book of Mormon record.

Appendix I gives a description of the metal plates from which the Book of Mormon was translated, and also another set of plates that were "sealed."

Finally, in the process of assembling these biographies, I became aware of some interesting relationships, viewpoints, and feelings concerning the Book of Mormon and some of its leading characters. A few of these impressions are included in Appendix II.

I knew that the Book of Mormon was a true record before I began this biographical work over twenty years ago. However, in compiling each biography, I was many times impressed with the intricacy of the story and the variety of names and events, and also with the number of unnamed persons who weave in and out of the general narrative. The complexity of the Book of Mormon is a witness to its historicity. But of even greater influence has been the witness of the Spirit that the record is of divine inspiration. It is a record of fact and a revelation from God. The greatness of the book was again and again impressed upon me.

Although I feel that the statements and conclusions that are made in this volume are correct, I wish to point out that this publication is a private endeavor, and I alone am responsible for the views expressed herein.

PART 1

ANALYTICAL BIOGRAPHIES

AARON—middle Jaredite
1. Descendant (possibly son) of Heth .... Ether 1:16; 10:31
2. Dwelt in captivity all his days .... Ether 10:31
3. Begat Amnigaddah .... Ether 10:31; 1:15

AARON—son of Mosiah—about B.C. 100
1. Unbeliever of things of God .... Mosiah 27:8, 34
2. Converted by angel that visited Alma .... Mosiah 27:32; Alma 17:2
3. Preached the gospel in Zarahemla .... Mosiah 27:32-37
4. Desired to preach to Lamanites .... Mosiah 28:1-9
5. Refused to succeed his father as king .... Mosiah 29:2-3; 28:10
6. In borders of Lamanite country, separated from brethren
   and traveled to land of Jerusalem .... Alma 21:2
7. Preached to Amalekites in city Jerusalem and village
   Ani-Anti .... Alma 21:4-10
8. Met Muloki, Ammah, and brethren at Ani-Anti .... Alma 21:11
9. Rejected—goes to land Middoni .... Alma 21:12
10. Imprisoned at Middoni .... Alma 21:13
11. Delivered from prison by Ammon (his brother) and Lamoni ..... Alma 21:14
12. Led by the Spirit to land Nephi .... Alma 22:1
13. Entered palace, conversed with Lamanite king (father
    of Lamoni) whom Ammon had confounded .... Alma 22:1-2
14. Presented plan of redemption beginning to end .... Alma 22:12-18
15. Raised the king who had fallen to earth .... Alma 22:17-23
16. Returned with Ammon to land Zarahemla .... Alma 27:16-19; 17:1-2
17. Rebuked his brother Ammon for "boasting" .... Alma 26:10
18. Went with Ammon and Alma to the Zoramites .... Alma 31:6-7
19. Without purse or script .... Alma 31:37-38
20. Returned to Zarahemla with Ammon and company .... Alma 35:14
21. Instrument in bringing Zoramites to repentance .... Alma 35:14
22. Consulted by king in naming Anti-Nephi-Lehis .... Alma 23:16

AARON—king of Lamanites—A.D. 330 and 385
1. King of the Lamanites .... Mormon 2:9
2. Leader of Lamanite army numbering 44,000 .... Mormon 2:9
3. Defeated by Mormon's Nephite army of 42,000 .... Mormon 2:9
4. Sent epistle to Mormon (some question as to identity) .... Mormon 3:4
5. Received dissenters from Nephites in last great struggle .... Moroni 9:17

1

ABINADI—about B.C. 150

1. Man in the kingdom of Noah .... Mosiah 11:20
2. Preached repentance to Noah's people .... Mosiah 11:20-25
3. Fled when Noah's people sought to kill him .... Mosiah 11:26
4. After two years, returned in disguise .... Mosiah 12:1
5. Preached destruction upon Noah's people .... Mosiah 12:1-8
6. Taken before king and accused of law breaking .... Mosiah 12:9-16
7. Cast into prison .... Mosiah 12:17
8. Brought before council of Noah's wicked priests ...... Mosiah 12:17-18
9. Confounded the priests; preached repentance, Christ's
   coming .... Mosiah 12:19; 16:15
10. Protected by the Lord—face shone like unto Moses' .... Mosiah 13:5
11. Taken again before the king and accused .... Mosiah 17:7
12. Condemned to die because he said Christ is God ..... Mosiah 17:7-10; 7:26
13. Refused to deny his words to save his life .... Mosiah 17:9-10
14. Burned to death with faggots .... Mosiah 17:13-20
15. Predicted retribution upon people of Noah for their sins;
    specified death by fire .... Mosiah 17:14-19
16. His words fulfilled .... Mosiah 20:21; Mormon 1:19

ABINADOM—between B.C. 279-130

1. Son of Chemish .... Omni 10
2. Had killed many Lamanites by sword in defense .... Omni 10
3. Mentioned the record kept by the kings .... Omni 11
4. Knew of no revelation besides that already written .... Omni 11
5. Made an end of writing .... Omni 11

ABISH—about B.C. 90

1. Lamanitish woman; servant of Lamoni .... Alma 19:16
2. Was converted unto the Lord on account of remarkable
   vision of her father .... Alma 19:16-17
3. Had never made her conversion known .... Alma 19:17
4. Saw that Ammon, Lamoni, the queen, and all the servants
   of Lamoni (except herself) had fallen by power of God .... Alma 19:17
5. Used opportunity to bring many people (she hoped) to
   know power of God; ran from house to house telling of the
   situation of Lamoni, queen, servants, and Ammon .... Alma 19:17
6. Was sorrowful unto tears when multitude caused dissention
   concerning Ammon .... Alma 19:28
7. Touched hand of queen; raised her from the ground .... Alma 19:29

AHA—about B.C. 80

1. Went with father Zoram, brother Lehi, to rescue captured
   brethren from the Lamanites (successful) .... Alma 16:5-8

AHAH—middle Jaredite

1. Son of Seth .... Ether 1:10; 11:10
2. Obtained possession of kingdom all his days .... Ether 11:10
3. Did much iniquity; shed much blood .... Ether 11:10
4. Few were his days .... Ether 11:10
5. Succeeded in office by Ethem, a descendant (son?) .... Ether 11:11; 1:9

2

AKISH — middle Jaredite
1. Son of Kimnor .... Ether 8:10
2. Friend of Omer, the king .... Ether 8:11
3. Desired daughter of Jared for a wife .... Ether 8:11
4. Gathered friends and kinfolk, whom he placed under oath
   to support him in obtaining death of Omer .... Ether 8:13-14
5. Instituted oaths and covenants handed down from Cain ...... Ether 8:15-19
6. Overthrew kingdom of Omer, but unable to slay him .... Ether 9:1-2
7. Married daughter of Jared (her name not given) .... Ether 9:4
8. Slew Jared (father-in-law) as he sat upon throne .... Ether 9:5-6
9. Reigned as king .... Ether 9:6
10. Jealous of own son—imprisoned and starved him to death
    (son's name not given) .... Ether 9:7
11. Desirous of gain and power .... Ether 9:11
12. Lost kingdom through rebellion of his sons (sons' names
    not given) .... Ether 9:10-12

ALMA, the elder—B.C. 173-91 (lived 82 years)
1. Priest of King Noah .... Mosiah 17:1-2; 24:9
2. Descendant of Nephi .... Mosiah 17:2
3. Young man .... Mosiah 17:2
4. Believed words of prophet Abinadi .... Mosiah 17:2; 26:15
5. Cast out by king, who also tried to kill him ...... Mosiah 17:3
6. Wrote all the words of Abinadi's preaching .... Mosiah 17:4
7. Repented of all sins and iniquity .... Mosiah 18:1
8. Privately taught Abinadi's words .... Mosiah 18:1-3
9. Resorted to place of Mormon, where are trees, water .... Mosiah 18:4-7
10. Baptized those who believed (about 204) .... Mosiah 18:8-16
11. Organized Church of Christ, ordained priests, at place
    called Mormon .... Mosiah 18:17-30; 3 Nephi 5:12
12. Took 450 people and fled into wilderness away from
    King Noah .... Mosiah 18:32-35
13. His whereabouts not known by Ammon and King Limhi's
    people (the people from whom he had fled) .... Mosiah 21:30-31
14. Escaped armies of Noah .... Mosiah 23:1-5
15. Refused to be king over his people .... Mosiah 23:6-15
16. High priest of the Church .... Mosiah 23:16-18
17. Exhorted people to trust Lord; not fear Lamanites .... Mosiah 23:26-27
18. Persecuted by priests of Noah, who in meantime had joined
    the Lamanites .... Mosiah 24:8-9
19. Led people to freedom from Amulon and Lamanites ...... Mosiah 24:18-25
20. United his people with people of Mosiah .... Mosiah 24:18-25
21. Preached repentance to all assembled people of Mosiah ..... Mosiah 25:15
22. Baptized Limhi and all his people .... Mosiah 25:17-18
23. Established Church throughout Zarahemla .... Mosiah 25:19-24
24. Instructed of Lord concerning wrong-doers and
    unbelievers .... Mosiah 26:14-33
25. Promised eternal life by voice of Lord .... Mosiah 26:20
26. Died at age 82 .... Mosiah 29:45
27. Founder of the church .... Mosiah 29:47

ALMA, son of Alma—probably born before B.C. 125; lived until B.C. 73

1. Unbeliever .... Mosiah 27:8
2. Wicked and idolatrous man .... Mosiah 27:8
3. Visited by angel, commanded to repent .... Mosiah 27:11-16
4. Unable to speak for two days after .... Mosiah 27:19-22
5. Unable to move hands, completely helpless .... Mosiah 27:19-22
6. Revived by faith and prayer of father and priests .... Mosiah 27:22-23
7. Taught gospel to the people .... Mosiah 27:32
8. Appointed 1st and chief judge of people of
   Zarahemla after Mosiah's death (B.C. 91) .... Mosiah 29:42-44
9. Sentenced Nehor to death for killing Gideon .... Alma 1:14-15
10. Led army against Amlicites .... Alma 2:16
11. Slew Amlici with the sword .... Alma 2:29-31
12. Fought, but did not slay, king of Lamanites .... Alma 2:32
13. Consecrated high priest of Church, by his father .... Alma 4:4; 5:3
14. Baptized many people .... Alma 4:4; 5:3
15. Relinquished judgment seat to Nephihah to allow
    more time for church .... Alma 4:16-19
16. Preached repentance to city Zarahemla .... Alma 5:2
17. Set church at Zarahemla in order; traveled to city Gideon .... Alma 6:7-8
18. Preached concerning birth and ministry of Christ to
    people in Gideon .... Alma 7:7-13
19. Preached to people of land Melek—success .... Alma 8:4-5
20. Traveled to city Ammonihah .... Alma 8:6
21. Rejected by city Ammonihah—leaves city .... Alma 8:8-13
22. Comforted by angel—told to return to city .... Alma 8:14-17
23. Fed by Amulek, a Nephite of city Ammonihah ...... Alma 8:19-22
24. Commanded by Lord to preach again to Ammonihahites .... Alma 8:29
25. Rejected the second time .... Alma 9:1-33
26. Preached to Zeezrom the lawyer, and others .... Alma 12:1-37; 13:1-31
27. Taken with Amulek before the chief judge .... Alma 14:4-5
28. Forced to watch many believers suffer death by fire
    at hands of Ammonihahites .... Alma 14:9-11
29. Cast into prison with Amulek many days .... Alma 14:17-24
30. Delivered by power of God—
    prison tumbled to earth .... Alma 14:25-29; 15:5-12; Ether 12:13
31. Healed lawyer Zeezrom from fever, baptized him .... Alma 15:5-12
32. Established church in land Sidon .... Alma 15:13-17
33. Returned to Zarahemla, accompanied by Amulek ...... Alma 15:18
34. Preached repentance to people of Nephites .... Alma 16:13-21
35. Met sons of Mosiah journeying to Zarahemla on their
    return from Lamanite mission .... Alma 17:1
36. Took them to his home .... Alma 27:20
37. Returned to wilderness with Ammon (son of Mosiah) to see
    people of Anti-Nephi-Lehi .... Alma 27:25
38. Settled Anti-Nephi-Lehis in land Jershon .... Alma 27:26-30
39. Rejoiced in success—Psalm of Alma .... Alma 29:1-17
40. Encountered Korihor the anti-Christ .... Alma 30:29
41. Confounded sign-seeking Korihor .... Alma 30:43-50
42. Took company to visit Zoramites (apostate Nephites) .... Alma 31:1-8
43. Traveled without purse or script .... Alma 31:37-38

4

44. Preached in Zoramite streets, synagogues, homes; little
    success .... Alma 32:1
45. Retired to land of Jershon .... Alma 34:1
46. Returned with group to Zarahemla .... Alma 35:14
47. Gave sons instructions in righteousness:
    Helaman, eldest son .... Alma 37
    Shiblon .... Alma 38
    Corianton .... Alma 39 to 42
48. May have seen God, even as father Lehi did .... Alma 36:22
49. With his sons, went forth to preach in Zarahemla .... Alma 43:1
50. Inquired of Lord about fighting with Lamanites; received
    answer as to Lamanite's location .... Alma 43:24
51. Prophesied (to Helaman) of Nephites' extinction in 4th
    generation after Christ .... Alma 45:2-14
52. Blessed all his sons .... Alma 45:15
53. Blessed the earth for the righteous .... Alma 45:15
54. Cursed the land (America) for the wicked's sake .... Alma 45:16
55. Departed Zarahemla toward land Melek; never heard of again .. Alma 45:18
56. Probably translated (B.C. 73) .... Alma 45:19

AMALEKI, son of Abinadom—between B.C. 279-130
1. Made comment about Mosiah .... Omni 1:12-23
2. Made comment about Benjamin, son of Mosiah .... Omni 1:23-24
3. Delivered small plates to Benjamin .... Omni 1:25
4. Mentioned a certain number of men lost in wilderness .... Omni 1:27-29
5. Had no children .... Omni 1:25
   *Note: AMALEKI must have traveled with Mosiah, leaving land of Nephi to go
   to Zarahemla. If so, the small plates were carried to Zarahemla by Amaleki
   and there given to King Benjamin, who in turn combined the records of the
   kings (large plates) with them.*

AMALICKIAH—about B.C. 50
1. Large, strong man; leader of rebellion against the church .... Alma 46:3
2. Desired to be king; flattered judges and people .... Alma 46:4-6
3. Man of cunning device and flattering words .... Alma 46:10
4. When opposed by Moroni, fled with followers to land
   Nephi (from Zarahemla) .... Alma 46:29-33
5. Stirred up Lamanites against Nephites .... Alma 47:1
6. Was made leader of Lamanite army by Lamanite king .... Alma 47:3-5
7. Devised plan to dethrone king of Lamanites .... Alma 47:4
8. Sought favor of the king's people, to gain power .... Alma 47:8
9. Betrayed his own army to become 2nd leader of a
   larger force .... Alma 47:13-15
10. Slew chief leader by poison; was appointed (according
    to custom) as successor—according to his scheme .... Alma 47:17-19
11. Marched with his united army into city of Nephi to see
    king of Lamanites .... Alma 47:20-21
12. Had king slain by deception and trickery .... Alma 47:22-26
13. Pretended to be wroth and surprised at king's death .... Alma 47:27-28
14. Sends men to capture the king's servants .... Alma 47:32
15. Informed the queen of death of the king .... Alma 47:32
16. Produced false witnesses to convince queen of king's death . Alma 47:33-34

5

17. Married the queen .... Alma 47:35
18. Became acknowledged king among all Lamanites, who were
    combination of Lamanites, Lemuelites, Ishmaelites, and
    dissenters of the Nephites .... Alma 47:35
19. Propagandized against the Nephites .... Alma 48:1
20. Sought to be king over Nephites as well as Lamanites .... Alma 48:2
21. Appointed Zoramites as captains of armies because of
    their knowledge and skill (see Alma 43:6) .... Alma 48:5
22. Moved his armies toward Zarahemla, but did not go
    with them .... Alma 48:6; 49:10
23. A Nephite by birth .... Alma 49:25
24. Very angry when his armies not conquer Nephites .... Alma 49:26
25. Cursed God, swore with oath to drink Moroni's blood .... Alma 49:27
26. Gathered army and personally went against Nephites
    (after five years) .... Alma 51:9-12
27. Conquered city Moroni and 6 other cities by east shore ..... Alma 51:23-24
28. Conquered many cities, slew many Nephites .... Alma 51:27-28
29. Battled with Teancum in land Bountiful .... Alma 51:29
30. Slain by Teancum while asleep in tent .... Alma 33:34

AMARON, son of Omni—B.C. 279
1. Wrote a little upon plates .... Omni 1:4
2. Delivered plates to his brother Chemish .... Omni 1:8
3. Wrote with own hand—no secretary .... Omni 1:9

AMGID—early Jaredite
1. King over Jaredites .... Ether 10:32
2. Conquered by Com .... Ether 10:32

AMINADAB—B.C. 30
1. Nephite dissenter .... Helaman 5:35
2. Had belonged to church of God .... Helaman 5:35
3. Witnessed circle of fire surrounding Nephi, Lehi;
   also their shining faces .... Helaman 5:36
4. Told multitude to look at faces of Lehi and Nephi .... Helaman 5:37
5. Told multitude that Lehi and Nephi conversed with
   the angels of God .... Helaman 5:38-39
6. Taught multitude that repentance was the means to
   remove cloud of darkness .... Helaman 5:40-41

AMINADI—between B.C. 600 and B.C. 80
1. Interpreted writings upon wall of Nephite temple as
   written by finger of God .... Alma 10:2
2. Descendant of Nephi son of Lehi .... Alma 10:3
3. Ancestor of a man named Ishmael .... Alma 10:2

AMLICI—about B.C. 80
1. Cunning man of the order of Nehor .... Alma 2:1
2. Aspired to be king in Zarahemla .... Alma 2:2
3. Rejected by the people .... Alma 2:6-7
4. Organized Amlicites and made war against people
   of Zarahemla .... Alma 2:9-11

5. Joined forces with the Lamanites .... Alma 2:24
6. Fought with Alma face to face with the sword .... Alma 2:29
7. Slain by Alma .... Alma 2:31

AMMAH—about B.C. 90
1. Imprisoned, land Middoni, with Aaron, Muloki .... Alma 20:2-3
2. Preached the word to people at village Ani-Anti with
   Muloki and the brethren (before imprisonment) .... Alma 21:11
3. Departed from Ani-Anti and went to land Middoni with
   Muloki and Aaron—imprisoned there .... Alma 21:11-12
4. Bound with cords, suffered much hunger, thirst .... Alma 20:29-30
5. Released and fed by Ammon, Lamoni .... Alma 20:28; 21:14

AMMON—about B.C. 100
1. Unbeliever, son of Mosiah .... Mosiah 27:8, 34
2. Converted by the angel that visited Alma,
   others .... Mosiah 27:32; Alma 17:2
3. Preached gospel in Zarahemla .... Mosiah 27:32-37
4. Desired a mission to the Lamanites .... Mosiah 28:1-9
5. Met Alma as he (Ammon) was returning from 14 years
   preaching to Lamanites .... Alma 17:1-4
6. Had gone to preach to Lamanites in first year of
   judges (B.C. 91) .... Alma 17:6
7. Separated from his brethren, according to plan .... Alma 17:13-18
8. Journeyed to land Ishmael .... Alma 17:19
9. Taken by Lamanites before King Lamoni .... Alma 17:20-21
10. Refused offer to marry daughter of Lamanite king .... Alma 17:24
11. Chose to be servant of King Lamoni .... Alma 17:25
12. Guarded king's flock from Lamanite aggressors .... Alma 17:25-38
13. On third day of duty smote off arms of Lamanites who
    came to scatter king's flocks .... Alma 17:37-39
14. Mistaken for the Great Spirit by the king .... Alma 18:2-4, 11
15. Taught gospel to the king who became overcome by
    the Spirit and fainted .... Alma 18:22-43
16. Called by queen to see if king dead or not .... Alma 19:2-10
17. Told queen that king overcome by spirit; not dead .... Alma 19:8
18. Sank to earth, overcome with Spirit and joy .... Alma 19:14
19. Protected by Lord from one who would have killed him
    while he lay overcome from Spirit .... Alma 19:21-23
20. Mistaken as the Great Spirit, by some .... Alma 19:25
21. Called a "monster" by others .... Alma 19:26
22. Arose and taught gospel to the people .... Alma 19:33
23. Instructed by Lord to go to land Middoni to free his brethren
    from prison .... Alma 20:2-3
24. Confounded Lamoni's father (chiefest Lamanite king)
    and obtained freedom of brethren from prison .... Alma 20:20-30
25. Returned with Lamoni to land of Ishmael .... Alma 21:18
26. Taught righteousness to people of Ishmael .... Alma 22:1-4
27. "Boasts" of goodness of God .... Alma 26:1-37
28. Rebuked mildly by Aaron for boasting .... Alma 26:10
29. Desired to take Anti-Nephi-Lehis to Zarahemla to live
    with Nephites .... Alma 27:4-5

7

30. Traveled with his brethren to investigate situation among Nephites, regarding Anti-Nephi-Lehis .... Alma 27:15-16
31. While traveling, met Alma (see item No. 5) .... Alma 27:16
32. Visited in Alma's home in Zarahemla .... Alma 27:20
33. Made the high priest of Anti-Nephi-Lehis (also called people of Ammon) in land Jershon .... Alma 30:20
34. Had Korihor (anti-Christ) removed from Jershon .... Alma 30:21
35. Went with Alma on mission to Zoramites (apostates) .... Alma 31:6-8
36. Trusted in Lord for all needs .... Alma 31:37-38
37. Returned with others to land of Jershon .... Alma 35:1
38. Returned with brethren and Zoramite converts to land Jershon and then to Zarahemla .... Alma 35:14
39. A man of God .... Alma 48:18

AMMON—about 121 B.C.
1. Strong and mighty man .... Mosiah 7:3
2. Descendant of Zarahemla .... Mosiah 7:3-13
3. Leader of expedition from Zarahemla to find land of Lehi-Nephi and people of Zeniff .... Mosiah 7:2, 3, 13
4. With Amaleki, Helem, Hem, taken prisoner by Limhi, king of land Nephi .... Mosiah 7:6-8; Helaman 5:21
5. Taught people of King Limhi concerning people of Zarahemla, and King Benjamin's address .... Mosiah 8:8-11
6. Learned of 24 gold plates with engravings found by people of King Limhi .... Mosiah 8:8-11
7. Discoursed on calling and office of a seer .... Mosiah 8:13-18
8. Sorrowed over death by Lamanites of so many of Limhi's people .... Mosiah 21:29
9. Considered himself unworthy to baptize others .... Mosiah 21:33

AMMARON, brother of Amos—about A.D. 321
1. Brother of Amos and son of Amos .... 4 Nephi 47
2. Succeeded his brother Amos in keeping sacred record; about A.D. 305 .... 4 Nephi 47
3. Hid up record (by inspiration) about A.D. 320 .... 4 Nephi 48-49
4. Instructed Mormon about keeping of records .... Mormon 1:2
5. Hid records in land Antum in hill Shim .... Mormon 1:3; 2:17; 4:22

AMMORON—about B.C. 66
1. Brother of Amalickiah .... Alma 52:3; 54:16
2. Succeeded Amalickiah as king of Lamanites .... Alma 52:3; 54:16
3. Departed out of Zarahemla with armies to go to w. sea .... Alma 52:12
4. Desired exchange of prisoners with Moroni .... Alma 54:1
5. Angered at Moroni's counterproposal for prisoner exchange; threatened Nephite destruction .... Alma 54:16-19
6. Accused Moroni of murdering Amalickiah .... Alma 54:21-22
7. Descendant of Zoram the servant of Laban .... Alma 54:23
8. Ordered Lamanite army not to attack armies of Antipus and Helaman but to maintain holdings .... Alma 56:18-20
9. Sent epistle to Helaman stating conditions for prisoner exchange .... Alma 57:1

8

10. Received epistle from Helaman rejecting his proposal
    and stating Helaman's terms .... Alma 57:2
11. Rejected Helaman's proposal for prisoner exchange .... Alma 57:3
12. Surrendered city Antiparah to Helaman without fight .... Alma 57:4
13. Sent new men, supplies, to strengthen Lamanite army .... Alma 57:17
14. Went personally with army to land Moroni .... Alma 62:33
15. Slain by Teancum in tent by night .: .... Alma 62:36
16. Alerted servant before dying, which resulted in death
    of Teancum also .... Alma 62:36
17. Father of Tubaloth who succeeded him as king
    of Lamanites .... Helaman 1:16

AMNIGADDAH—middle Jaredite
1. Son of Aaron .... Ether 1:15; 10:31
2. Dwelt in captivity all his days .... Ether 10:31
3. Begat Coriantum .... Ether 10:31; 1:14

AMNOR—about B.C. 87
1. One of four spies sent by Alma to watch Amlicites
   (see Zeram, Manti, Limher) .... Alma 2:21-22
2. Returned with word that Amlicites, Lamanites coming .... Alma 2:23-26

AMORON—about A.D. 400-421
1. Nephite, sent word to Mormon concerning prisoners of
   war taken by Lamanites; their sufferings, etc. .... Moroni 9:7

AMOS, son of Nephi—about A.D. 110-194
1. Son of Nephi who was the son of Nephi .... 4 Nephi 19
2. Succeeded his father in keeping sacred record .... 4 Nephi 19
3. Kept record more than 84 years .... 4 Nephi 20
4. Died about year 194 A.D. .... 4 Nephi 21
5. Succeeded in record-keeping by son Amos .... 4 Nephi 21
6. Record of, incorporated in Book of Nephi .... 4 Nephi 21
   Note: Great age of this man, approximately 100 years or more.

AMOS, son of Amos—about A.D. 200-300
1. Son of Amos who was son of Nephi .... 4 Nephi 21
2. Succeeded his father in record keeping .... 4 Nephi 21
3. Died about year 305 A.D. .... 4 Nephi 47
4. Succeeded by his brother Ammaron .... 4 Nephi 47
   Note the great age of this man, well over 110 years.

AMULEK—about B.C. 80
1. Lived in city Ammonihah .... Alma 8:18-22
2. Told by angel to feed Alma the prophet .... Alma 8:20; 10:7-9
3. Commanded by Lord to preach repentance .... Alma 8:29
4. Descendant of Nephi, tribe of Manasseh .... Alma 10:2-3
5. Questioned by Zeezrom the lawyer .... Alma 11:21
6. Taught that men must be saved
   from sin, not in sin .... Alma 11:33-37; Helaman 5:10
7. Confounded Zeezrom .... Alma 11:46; 12:1

9

8. Taken with Alma before chief judge, falsely accused .... Alma 14:4-5
9. Forced to witness death by fire of believers .... Alma 14:9-14
10. With Alma, imprisoned, spit upon, mocked .... Alma 14:17-24
11. Delivered by power of God;
    prison tumbled to earth .... Alma 14:25-29; Ether 12:13
12. Forsook riches for the word of God .... Alma 15:16
13. Rejected and disowned by own father .... Alma 15:16
14. Traveled to Zarahemla with Alma .... Alma 15:18
15. Preached repentance extensively among Nephites .... Alma 16:13-21
16. Traveled with Alma and Mosiah's sons to Zoramites .... Alma 31:6-7
17. Preached vigorously to Zoramites about atonement .... Alma 34:1-41
18. Returned with the group to Zarahemla .... Alma 35:14

AMULON—about B.C. 150
1. Leader of priests of Noah .... Mosiah 23:31-32
2. With other priests joined with Lamanites .... Mosiah 23:35
3. Made governor and teacher over people of Alma by
   king of Lamanites .... Mosiah 23:39; 24:1
4. Persecuted Alma .... Mosiah 24:8-9
5. Taught Lamanites the Nephite language .... Mosiah 24:4
6. With other priests, kidnapped and married Lamanite girls .... Mosiah 20:3-5
7. Found favor with King Laman (the younger) .... Mosiah 24:1
   Note: See Alma 25:4-13 concerning the seed of Amulon and the
   prophecy of Abinadi.

ANTIOMNO—about B.C. 90
1. King of Middoni .... Alma 20:4
2. Friend of Lamoni .... Alma 20:4
3. Granted release of Aaron, Muloki, Ammah from prison .... Alma 20:2, 28

ANTIONAH
1. A chief ruler among the people of Ammonihah .... Alma 12:20
2. Questioned Alma about the resurrection .... Alma 12:20-21

ANTIONUM—about 385 A.D.
1. Nephite military leader with 10,000 at Cumorah .... Mormon 6:14
2. Slain in battle .... Mormon 6:14

ANTIPUS—about B.C. 65
1. Appointed leader of Nephite army in one part of land .... Alma 56:9
2. Joined by Helaman's 2000 young men .... Alma 56:9-10
3. Suffered many losses to Lamanite armies .... Alma 56:10
4. Toiled greatly to fortify city Judea .... Alma 56:15
5. Depressed in body, spirit, as result of afflictions .... Alma 56:16
6. Greatly cheered by Helaman's 2000 soldiers .... Alma 56:17
7. With Helaman, maintained constant vigil over Lamanites .... Alma 56:20-23
8. Gathered and commanded an army of 10,000 men .... Alma 56:28
9. Pursued Lamanite army which in turn pursued Helaman's ...... Alma 56:33
10. Slain in battle .... Alma 56:61
11. Men of, enabled to conquer Lamanites with Helaman's help . Alma 56:52-54
12. Men of (portion), marched Lamanite prisoners from Judea
    to land Zarahemla .... Alma 56:57

ANTI-NEPHI-LEHI'S—about B.C. 80 (Also known as people of Ammon)
1. Lamanites converted by sons of Mosiah . . . . Alma 23:16-17
2. After conversion would suffer death rather than commit sin . . . Alma 24:6-24
3. Given land Jershon, south of Zarahemla, by Nephites . . . . Alma 27:25-27
4. Became known as people of Ammon . . . . Alma 27:26
5. Made covenant not to take arms against brethren . . . . Alma 56:6
6. Were about to break covenant in emergency defense of country . Alma 56:7
7. Advised by Helaman not to break covenant . . . . Alma 56:8
8. Were parents of Helaman's 2000 young warriors . . . . Alma 56:5-6
9. Sent provisions, supplies to sons at battlefront . . . . Alma 56:27
10. Joined by 4000 additional Lamanites who had made
    similar oath . . . . Alma 62:17
11. Joined by many other Lamanite prisoners . . . . Alma 62:27-28
12. Many went into land northward in days of Helaman . . . . Helaman 3:12

ARCHEANTUS—about 385 A.D.
1. Nephite soldier slain in final struggle of Nephites . . . . Moroni 9:2

BENJAMIN, son of Mosiah 1—about B.C. 120
1. Son of Mosiah . . . . Omni 23
2. Succeeded Mosiah as king of Zarahemla . . . . Omni 23-24
3. Received record-plates from Amaleki . . . . Omni 25
4. Combined king-record with prophet-record . . . . W. of Mor. 10
5. Fought with own army against Lamanites . . . . W. of Mor. 13
6. Established peace in land Zarahemla . . . . Mosiah 1:1
7. Had 3 sons: Mosiah, Helorum, Helaman . . . . Mosiah 1:2
8. Asked Mosiah to gather people that he (Benjamin)
    could address them . . . . Mosiah 1:10
9. Delivered kingdom to son Mosiah . . . . Mosiah 1:10-15
10. Possessed brass plates, plates of Nephi, sword of
    Laban, Liahona. Instructed Mosiah concerning same . . . . Mosiah 1:16
11. Built tower on which to stand while speaking . . . . Mosiah 2:7
12. Addressed his people on numerous subjects . . . . Mosiah 2:9; 4:30;
                                                                          Helaman 5:9
13. Told of ministry of angel to him . . . . Mosiah 3:2-3; 4:1
14. Died about B.C. 121 . . . . Mosiah 6:5

CAIN—son of Adam
1. Received encouragement from Satan to murder Abel . . . . Helaman 6:27
2. Was promised by Satan that murder of Abel would not be
    known unto world . . . . Helaman 6:27
3. A murderer from the beginning . . . . Ether 8:15

CAMENIHAH—about 385 B.C.
1. Nephite military leader with 10,000 men at Cumorah . . . . Mormon 6:14
2. Slain in battle . . . . Mormon 6:14

CEZORAM—about B.C. 30 (wicked man)
1. Succeeded Nephi in judgment seat . . . . Helaman 5:1

11

2. Murdered after about 4 years' reign by an unknown
   hand while on judgment seat .... Helaman 6:15
3. Murdered by one of Gadianton's band .... Helaman 6:19

CHEMISH, son of Omni—between B.C. 279-130
1. Brother of Amoron .... Omni 1:8
2. Wrote but very little .... Omni 1:9
3. Observed Amoron write with own hand .... Omni 1:9
   Note: Chemish seems to have written the least of any author in the Book of Mormon record.

COHOR—early Jaredite
1. Son of Noah .... Ether 7:19-21
2. King over one part of the Jaredites .... Ether 7:20
3. Slain by army of Shule .... Ether 7:21
4. Father of Nimrod .... Ether 7:22

COM—early Jaredite
1. Son of king Coriantum .... Ether 1:27; 9:24-5
2. Succeeded his father as king .... Ether 9:25
3. Reigned 49 years .... Ether 9:25
4. Begat Heth .... Ether 9:25
5. Begat other sons and daughter .... Ether 9:25
6. Dethroned and slain by son Heth .... Ether 9:27
7. Succeeded as king by son Heth .... Ether 9:27

COM—late Jaredite
1. Son of Coriantum .... Ether 1:13; 10:32
2. Drew away half the kingdom .... Ether 10:32
3. Reigned over half the kingdom for 42 years .... Ether 10:32
4. Went to battle against King Amgid .... Ether 10:32
5. Obtained full kingdom .... Ether 10:32
6. Fought against influence of robbers—not prevail .... Ether 10:34
7. Aided and believed prophets who came to him for protection .. Ether 11:1-3
8. Lived to good old age .... Ether 11:4
9. Begat Shiblom .... Ether 11:4
10. Succeeded in throne by Shiblom .... Ether 11:4
    Note: Varied spelling of Shiblom/Shiblon in Ether 11:4; 1:13 which are no doubt the same person

CORIANTON, son of Alma—about B.C. 75
1. Accompanied Alma, others, to Zoramite mission .... Alma 31:6-8
2. Blessed by Alma .... Alma 45:15
3. Did not follow father's counsel faithfully .... Alma 39:2
4. Forsook ministry to follow harlot Isabel .... Alma 39:3
5. Boasted in own strength and wisdom .... Alma 39:2
6. Marveled (questioned?) why knowledge of Christ should be
   had before his coming .... Alma 39:17
7. Was worried about resurrection of the dead .... Alma 40:1
8. Worried about justice of God in punishment of sinner ... Alma 42:1
9. Worried about restoration and justice .... Alma 41:1
10. Called to God to preach to people .... Alma 42:31

12

11. Had been ordained and baptized .... Alma 49:30
12. Sailed into north countries to carry provisions .... Alma 63:10

CORIANTOR—late Jaredite
1. Son of Moron .... Ether 1:7; 11:18
2. Dwelt in captivity all his days .... Ether 11:19
3. Begat Ether as son or descendant (cf. 1:6) .... Ether 11:23
4. Died, after life of captivity .... Ether 11:23

CORIANTUM—early Jaredite
1. Son of king Emer .... Ether 1:28; 9:21
2. Anointed king by, and to succeed, his father .... Ether 9:21
3. Builder of cities .... Ether 9:23
4. A good king .... Ether 9:23
5. Had not children until exceedingly old .... Ether 9:23
6. Wife died, being 102 years old .... Ether 9:24
7. In old age, married young maid .... Ether 9:24
8. Begat sons and daughters .... Ether 9:24
9. Lived until 142 years of age .... Ether 9:24
10. Begat Com, who reigned in his stead .... Ether 9:25

CORIANTUM—middle Jaredite
1. Son of Amnigaddah .... Ether 1:13; 10:31
2. Dwelt in captivity all his days .... Ether 10:31
3. Begat Com .... Ether 10:31; 1:13

CORIANTUMR—about B.C. 51
1. Lamanite military leader .... Helaman 1:15
2. Dissenter from Nephites .... Helaman 1:15
3. Descendant of Zarahemla .... Helaman 1:15
4. Large and mighty man .... Helaman 1:15-16
5. Much wisdom .... Helaman 1:16
6. Appointed military leader by Tubaloth, Lamanite king ..... Helaman 1:16-17
7. With great army captured city of Zarahemla .... Helaman 1:18-20
8. Slew Pacumeni the chief judge .... Helaman 1:21
9. Led large army toward Bountiful with intent to
   capture Nephites in that area .... Helaman 1:23
10. Captured many important Nephite cities .... Helaman 1:24-27
11. Was defeated and slain by armies of Lehi, Moronihah ..... Helaman 1:28-32

CORIANTUMR—early Jaredite
1. Born in captivity, son of King Omer .... Ether 8:4
2. With brother Esrom, rescued kingdom from Jared and
   restored Omer (father) to throne .... Ether 8:5-6
3. Spared Jared from death .... Ether 8:6

CORIANTUMR—late Jaredite
1. King of Jaredites .... Ether 12:1
2. Lived in days of Ether the prophet .... Ether 12:2
3. Pursued by many who wished to destroy him .... Ether 13:15, 18
4. Studied arts of war and cunning of world .... Ether 13:16
5. Gave battle to enemies .... Ether 13:16

13

6. Himself, nor sons and daughters not repentant .... Ether 13:17
7. Sons of, fought much and bled much .... Ether 13:19
8. Warned by Lord, through Ether, to repent or be destroyed
and see another people inherit the land .... Ether 13:20-21
9. To receive burial by another people .... Ether 13:21
10. To be sole survivor of his people .... Ether 13:21
11. Captured by Shared .... Ether 13:23
12. Received kingdom again through aid of sons .... Ether 13:24
13. Fought again with Shared, both beating him and being
beaten by him .... Ether 13:27-29
14. Slew Shared in valley of Gilgal .... Ether 13:30
15. Wounded in thigh by Shared .... Ether 13:31
16. After 2 years, attacked and eventually beaten by
brother of Shared .... Ether 14:3-6
17. Gathered strength for two years to army .... Ether 14:7
18. Fought with and was wounded on arm by Lib .... Ether 14:10-12
19. Slew Lib .... Ether 14:16
20. Fought against Shiz, brother of Lib .... Ether 14:17-18
21. Fled from Shiz, who had sworn to avenge death of Lib .... Ether 14:24
22. Could not be slain because of word of Lord that he
(Coriantumr) would live to be last Jaredite .... Ether 14:24
23. Wounded severely by Shiz; fainted from loss of
blood—seemingly dead .... Ether 14:30
24. Began to repent of evils .... Ether 15:3
25. Wrote epistle to Shiz, offering kingdom to end war .... Ether 15:4
26. When offer was rejected fled from army of Shiz .... Ether 15:6-7
27. Wounded again in battle with Shiz .... Ether 15:9
28. Wrote 2nd epistle to Shiz; offer kingdom to end war .... Ether 15:18
29. After six days of battle, smote off head of Shiz .... Ether 15:20-30
30. Fell to earth as though dead .... Ether 15:32
31. Lived with people of Zarahemla nine moons .... Omni 21

CORIHOR—early Jaredite
1. Son of Kib .... Ether 7:3
2. When 32, rebelled against father and dwelt in Nehor .... Ether 7:4
3. Begat sons and daughters .... Ether 7:4
4. Overthrew father (Kib) and obtained kingdom .... Ether 7:5
5. Was in turn overthrown by brother Shule .... Ether 7:8-9
6. After repentance, given power in Shule's kingdom .... Ether 7:13
7. Many sons, daughters, including Noah, Cohor .... Ether 7:14
8. Sons and daughters of, not repentant .... Ether 13:17

COROM—middle Jaredite
1. Son of King Levi .... Ether 1:20; 10:16
2. Anointed by father to be king .... Ether 10:16
3. Good king .... Ether 10:17
4. Begat many sons and daughters .... Ether 10:17
5. Died after many days .... Ether 10:17
6. Succeeded by son Kish .... Ether 10:17; 1:19

EMER—early Jaredite
1. Son of Omer .... Ether 9:14

14

2. Anointed king by his father .... Ether 9:14
3. Reigned for approximately 62 years .... Ether 9:16
4. Administered judgment in righteousness .... Ether 9:21
5. Begat many sons and daughters .... Ether 9:21
6. Anointed son Coriantum to reign in stead .... Ether 9:21
7. Lived 4 years after anointing Coriantum .... Ether 9:22
8. Saw Son of Righteousness .... Ether 9:22
9. Died in peace .... Ether 9:22

EMRON—about A.D. 385
1. Nephite soldier slain in last struggle .... Moroni 9:2

ENOS, son of Jacob—about B.C. 500
1. Promised obedience to father Jacob's commands about
   care of sacred records .... Jacob 7:27
2. Was taught language of his father .... Enos 1
3. Taught nurture and admonition of Lord by father .... Enos 1
4. Had "wrestle" before God before obtaining remission .... Enos 2
5. Hunted wild beasts in forests .... Enos 3
6. Soul hungered for righteousness .... Enos 4
7. Kneeled in prayer; prayed for own soul all day, night .... Enos 4
8. Heard voice of Lord; received remission of sins .... Enos 5-7
9. Had never before heard or seen Christ .... Enos 8
10. Felt desire for welfare of Nephites .... Enos 9-10
11. Felt desire for welfare of Lamanites .... Enos 11-12
12. Desired that record of Nephites be preserved and be
    given to Lamanites at some future time .... Enos 13-17
13. Testified of things heard and seen .... Enos 19
14. Gave description of Lamanite life and culture .... Enos 20
15. Gave description of Nephite life and culture .... Enos 21
16. Stated that many Lamanites ate nothing but raw meat .... Enos 20
17. Saw wars between Lamanites and Nephites .... Enos 24
18. Began to be old; knew he would see face of Redeemer
    with pleasure .... Enos 27
19. Rejoiced in truth of Christ above that of world .... Enos 26
20. Commanded son Jarom to keep the record .... Jarom 1

ESROM—early Jaredite
1. Son of Omer .... Ether 8:3-4
2. Born while father was in captivity to another son, Jared ..... Ether 8:4
3. With Coriantumr (brother) overthrew Jared's army
   and restored father to throne .... Ether 8:5-6
4. Spared Jared from death .... Ether 8:6

ETHEM—late Jaredite (wicked king)
1. Son of Ahah .... Ether 1:9; 11:11
2. Obtained the kingdom .... Ether 11:11
3. Wicked king .... Ether 11:14
4. Begat Moron, who succeeded him in the kingdom .... Ether 11:14

ETHER—late Jaredite
1. Son (or descendant) of Coriantor .... Ether 1:6; 11:23

2. Lived in days of King Coriantumr .... Ether 12:1
3. Prophet, with Spirit of the Lord .... Ether 12:2
4. Preached morning until evening—faith, repentance .... Ether 12:3
5. Prophesied great, marvelous things which people
did not believe .... Ether 12:5
6. Told people all things from beginning of man .... Ether 13:1
7. Taught concerning New, Old Jerusalems .... Ether 13:3-12
8. Cast out by people .... Ether 13:13
9. Dwelt in cavity of rock by day .... Ether 13:13, 14, 18, 22
10. Viewed people's activities by night .... Ether 13:13
11. While in cavity of rock made historical record .... Ether 13:14
12. Had to flee for life .... Ether 13:22
13. Observed final battle between Coriantumr, Shiz .... Ether 15:13-33
14. Completed record and hid it in manner that people
of Limhi could find it .... Ether 15:33
15. Wondered whether would be translated or suffer death in flesh . Ether 15:34

EZIAS—ancient prophet
1. Ancient prophet; testified of coming of Son of God,
as quoted by Nephi .... Helaman 8:20
Note: Writings of Ezias were probably upon plates of brass.

GADIANTON—about B.C. 50
1. Exceeding expert in many words, murder, robbery .... Helaman 2:4
2. Became leader of band of Kishkumen .... Helaman 2:4
3. Sought by cunning and flattery to be appointed judge .... Helaman 2:5
4. Fled to wilderness to escape capture by Helaman's men ..... Helaman 2:11
5. Largely responsible for overthrow of Nephites .... Helaman 2:12-14
6. Established secret combinations in more settled parts
of the land .... Helaman 3:23
7. Band of, murdered Cezoram, the chief judge .... Helaman 6:15-19
8. Band of, murdered son of Cezoram,
newly appointed judge .... Helaman 6:15-19
9. Administerd secret oaths, laws, to his band .... Helaman 6:24
10. Received oaths, laws, signs, etc., from Satan .... Helaman 6:26
11. Band of, seduced people politically and obtained sole
management of the government .... Helaman 6:38-41
12. Supported more by Nephites than by Lamanites .... Helaman 6:38-41
Note: See entry on Gadianton robbers in Appendix.

GID—about B.C. 63
1. Nephite captain given charge of Lamanite prisoners of war ..... Alma 57:29
2. With his men, started on journey to take Lamanite
prisoners from Cumeni to Zarahemla .... Alma 57:13-16
3. Returned to battlefield next day—without prisoners, but
in time to assist Helaman's army in battle against Lamanites . Alma 57:18-22
4. Because of rebellion of prisoners, had had to
slay the greater portion of them .... Alma 57:28-33
5. Reported prisoner rebellion to Helaman .... Alma 57:28, 36
6. Was stationed with small band—for strategy—
in wilderness near city Manti (see Teomner) .... Alma 58:16-17

16

7. With Teomner, destroyed the Lamanite spies
   and guards at city Manti .... Alma 58:20-21

GIDDIANHI—about A.D. 16
1. Leader of secret society of Gadianton .... 3 Nephi 3:9
2. Sent epistle to chief judge Lachoneus .... 3 Nephi 3:1-10
3. Told Lachoneus to surrender Nephite lands and
   possessions peacefully or be destroyed .... 3 Nephi 3:7-8
4. Went to battle against Nephites in A.D. 19 .... 3 Nephi 4:5-6
5. Outfitted Gadianton robbers in lambskin dyed in
   blood, shorn heads, headplates .... 3 Nephi 4:7
6. Was defeated and slain by Nephites near land
   Zarahemla .... 3 Nephi 4:14; 3:23

GIDDONAH—before B.C. 80
1. Son of Ishmael who descended from Nephi through Aminadi ... Alma 10:2-3
2. Father of Amulek .... Alma 10:2
3. Rejected Amulek for taking up with Alma and word of God ..... Alma 15:16
4. Possibly a wealthy man .... Alma 15:16

GIDEON—about B.C. 150
1. Strong man in King Noah's army .... Mosiah 19:4
2. Started insurrection and attempted to slay Noah .... Mosiah 19:4
3. With drawn sword pursued Noah to top of tower .... Mosiah 19:4-6
4. Spared Noah's life when Lamanites attack city .... Mosiah 19:7-8
5. Sent men to pursue Noah, who had fled into wilderness ...... Mosiah 19:18
6. Received report from his men that Noah had been
   slain by his own people .... Mosiah 19:18-24
7. Suggested to King Limhi that it was the priests of
   Noah who had carried away daughters of Lamanites ...... Mosiah 20:17-18
8. Was captain in King Limhi's service .... Mosiah 20:17
9. Instrumental in pacifying Lamanites toward
   Limhi's people .... Mosiah 20:19-26
10. Devised plan for escape of Limhi's people by getting
    Lamanite guards drunk with wine .... Mosiah 22:3-9; Alma 1:8
11. Member and teacher in church of God .... Alma 1:5
12. Withstood Nehor (enemy of church) with word of God .... Alma 1:7
13. Old and stricken with years .... Alma 1:9
14. Slain by Nehor .... Alma 1:9
15. A righteous man .... Alma 1:13

GIDGIDDONAH—about A.D. 385
1. Nephite military leader with 10,000 men at Cumorah .... Mormon 6:13
2. Slain in battle .... Mormon 6:13

GIDGIDDONI—about A.D. 16
1. Chief captain and great commander of Nephite
   armies in days of Lachoneus .... 3 Nephi 3:18
2. Had spirit of revelation—a great prophet .... 3 Nephi 3:19
3. Warned Nephites about dangers of aggression .... 3 Nephi 3:21
4. Supervised the equipping of people with weapons, armor ..... 3 Nephi 3:23
5. Led Nephite armies in defeat of robbers .... 3 Nephi 4:8-15

17

6. Defeated many armies of robbers by stratagem . . . . 3 Nephi 4:24-26
7. Given credit, with Lachoneus, for establishing peace . . . . 3 Nephi 6:6

GILEAD—late Jaredite
1. Gave battle to Coriantumr but unsuccessful . . . . Ether 14:3
2. Fought again and obtained throne of Coriantumr . . . . Ether 14:4-6
3. Slain on the throne by his high priest . . . . Ether 14:9

GILGAH—early Jaredite
1. Son of Jared, declined persuadings of people to be king . . . . . Ether 6:14-27

GILGAL—about 385 A.D.
1. Nephite military leader with 10,000 men at Cumorah . . . . Mormon 6:14
2. Slain in battle . . . . Mormon 6:14

HAGOTH—about B.C. 53
1. Exceedingly curious man . . . . Alma 63:5
2. Built exceedingly large ship near land Bountiful . . . . Alma 63:5
3. Launched into west sea near narrow neck of land . . . . Alma 63:5
4. Built other ships which sailed into land northward, but did not
   return (whether Hagoth was a passenger is not recorded) . . . . . Alma 63:7-8

HEARTHOM—middle Jaredite
1. Son of Lib . . . . Ether 1:17; 10:29
2. Reigned in place of father . . . . Ether 10:30
3. Lost kingdom after reign of 24 years . . . . Ether 10:30
4. Served many years in captivity, until death . . . . Ether 10:30
5. Begat Heth . . . . Ether 10:31

HELAM—about B.C. 150
1. Believer, first to be baptized by Alma in waters of Mormon . Mosiah 18:12-15

HELAMAN, son of Alma—about B.C. 100-50
1. Eldest son of Alma . . . . Alma 31:7
2. Admonished, instructed by father . . . . Alma 36:1-30
3. Given sacred Nephite records . . . . Alma 37:1-2
4. Given plates of brass, and instructed concerning same . . . . Alma 37:3-10
5. Given twenty-four plates of Jaredites . . . . Alma 37:21-32
6. Given ''interpreters'' . . . . Alma 37:23-24
7. Given Liahona (compass or director) . . . . Alma 37:38-47
8. Given prophecy by Alma, of Nephite destruction;
   forbidden to reveal it except to write it in sacred records . . . . . . Alma 45:2-14
9. Blessed by Alma . . . . Alma 45:15
10. Ordained priests, teachers in Church . . . . Alma 45:22-23
11. Rejected by proud and rich . . . . Alma 45:23-24
12. High priest in Church; preached repentance . . . . Alma 46:6
13. Maintained peace for 4 years . . . . Alma 46:38
14. Very serviceable to people; preached, baptized . . . . Alma 48:19
15. Preached according to holy order of God . . . . Alma 49:30
16. Persuaded converted Lamanites to keep oaths . . . . Alma 53:10-15
17. Led 2000 young men to war . . . . Alma 53:22

18. Wrote epistle to Moroni, stating affairs of the people .... Alma 56:58
19. Cautioned people of Ammon not to break covenant .... Alma 56:7-8
20. Joined forces with Antipus against Lamanites .... Alma 56:9-20
21. Maintained (with Antipus) constant vigil over
    movements of Lamanites .... Alma 56:20-23
22. Gathered, commanded army of 10,000 men .... Alma 56:28
23. Led 2,000 young men to decoy Lamanites from city
    Antiparah .... Alma 56:30-36
24. Captured many Lamanite prisoners; sent to land Zarahemla .... Alma 56:57
25. Received Ammoron's epistle concerning prisoner exchange ..... Alma 57:1
26. Sent epistle to Ammoron rejecting proposal, and
    stated own terms for prisoner exchange .... Alma 57:2
27. Obtained city Antiparah from Lamanites without fight .... Alma 57:4
28. Captured city Cumeni by cutting off food supply .... Alma 57:7-12
29. Sent part of army to conduct abundance of
    Lamanite prisoners to Zarahemla .... Alma 57:13-17
30. Engaged in severe, victorious battle with Lamanites .... Alma 57:17-23
31. Received report from Gid concerning escape of
    Lamanite prisoners .... Alma 57:28-36
32. Praised God for his mercy, deliverance to Nephites .... Alma 57:36
33. By strategy arranged capture of Lamanite city
    Manti without shedding of blood .... Alma 58:1-28
34. Obtained release of many Nephite prisoners .... Alma 58:30-31
35. Praised God for protection, deliverance .... Alma 58:33
36. Wondered why government not send more men, provisions .. Alma 58:34-36
37. Received 6000 men, provisions, due to Moroni's intervention ... Alma 62:12
38. Returned to land Zarahemla with Moroni .... Alma 62:42
39. Began preaching tour to regulate Church .... Alma 62:44
40. Preached with power and authority .... Alma 62:45-46
41. Died during 35th year of judges B.C. 57 .... Alma 62:52
42. Kept sacred things till death .... Alma 63:1

HELAMAN, son of Helaman—about B.C. 100-40
1. Given charge of sacred things by uncle Shiblon .... Alma 63:11
2. Sent forth sacred writings throughout land .... Alma 63:12
3. Appointed to vacancy of judgment seat occasioned
   by murder of Pahoran .... Helaman 2:2
4. Pursued by Kishkumen who sought to slay him .... Helaman 2:3-6
5. Saved from death by servant .... Helaman 2:6-9
6. Being informed by murderous plot of Kishkumen, gave
   orders that secret band be tried and executed by law ...... Helaman 2:9-10
7. Filled judgment seat with justice, equity, righteousness ...... Helaman 3:20
8. Had 2 sons—Nephi (eldest); Lehi (youngest) .... Helaman 3:21
9. Died in 53rd year of judges (B.C. 39) .... Helaman 3:37
10. Succeeded in judgment seat by eldest son Nephi .... Helaman 3:37
11. Taught children; why named sons Lehi, Nephi;
    also testimony of Christ .... Helaman 5:5-13

HELEM—about B.C. 120
1. Went with 15 others on expedition from Zarahemla in
   search of land Lehi-Nephi .... Mosiah 7:6

19

2. Taken prisoner with Ammon, Amaleki, Hem, in Shilom . . . . Mosiah 7:7
   Note: Mosiah 7:7 may or may not indicate Helem to be a blood brother to Ammon.

HELORUM, son of King Benjamin—about B.C. 124
1. One of three sons . . . . Mosiah 1:2
2. Was taught in language and learning of father . . . . Mosiah 1:2

HEM—about B.C. 120
1. Went with 15 others on expedition from Zarahemla in
   search of land Lehi-Nephi . . . . Mosiah 7:6
2. Taken prisoner in land Shilom with Ammon, Amaleki, Helem . . . . Mosiah 7:7
   Note: Mosiah 7:6 may or may not indicate that Hem was blood brother to Ammon.

HETH—early Jaredite
1. Son of King Com . . . . Ether 1:26; 8:25
2. Embraced secret plans and wickedness of old . . . . Ether 9:26
3. Sought to destroy his father Com . . . . Ether 9:26
4. Dethroned, slew father with own sword . . . . Ether 9:27
5. Reigned as king in father's stead . . . . Ether 9:27
6. Sought to destroy prophets of the Lord . . . . Ether 9:28-29
7. Perished in famine sent by Lord as consequence of sin . . . . . . Ether 9:28-35
8. Succeeded as king by son Shez . . . . Ether 10:1

HETH—middle Jaredite
1. Son of Hearthom . . . . Ether 1:16; 10:31
2. Lived in captivity all his days . . . . Ether 10:31

HIMNI, son of Mosiah II—about B.C. 100-50
1. Unbeliever . . . . Mosiah 27:8, 34
2. Converted by angel that visited Alma (Al. 17:2) . . . . Mosiah 27:10, 32
3. Preached gospel in Zarahemla . . . . Mosiah 27:32-37
4. Desired a mission to Lamanites . . . . Mosiah 28:1-9
5. Met Alma when returning from 14 years among Lamanites . . . . . Alma 17:1-4
6. Had gone to Lamanite mission in 1st year of judges . . . . Alma 17:6
7. Separated from brethren according to plan . . . . Alma 17:13-18
8. Had refused the crown to be free to preach . . . . Alma 17:6
9. Presided over church in Zarahemla while Alma,
   Ammon, Aaron, Omner went to Zoramite mission . . . . Alma 31:6

ISABEL—about B.C. 75
1. Harlot in land of Siron; visited by Corianton . . . . Alma 39:3
2. Stole away the hearts of many . . . . Alma 39:4

ISAIAH, Hebrew Prophet—B.C. 740-200 (Plates of Brass)
1. Wrote unto all the house of Israel . . . . 1 Nephi 19:23-24; 2 Nephi 6:5
2. Wrote many things hard to be understood . . . . 2 Nephi 25:1-4
3. Writings of, understood by Spirit of prophecy . . . . 2 Nephi 25:4
4. Testified of coming of the Son of God . . . . Helaman 8:18-20
5. Great were the words of . . . . 3 Nephi 23:1

6. Wrote of all things pertaining to Israel and Gentiles . . . . 3 Nephi 23:2
7. All things he wrote and spake were true . . . . 3 Nephi 23:3
8. Writings of, should be searched . . . . 3 Nephi 23:1; Mormon 8:23.

ISAIAH—A.D. 33
1. One of the Twelve Disciples chosen by Jesus . . . . 3 Nephi 19:4
2. Present also in the group . . . . 3 Nephi 12:1, 28:1-3

ISHMAEL—B.C. 600
1. Persuaded by Nephi to leave Jerusalem with family
   and accompany Lehi's family in the wilderness . . . . 1 Nephi 7:2-5
2. Heart of, softened by the Lord . . . . 1 Nephi 7:5
3. Accompanied by wife, 2 sons, 5 daughters . . . . 1 Nephi 7:6
4. Daughters of, married Lehi's sons . . . . 1 Nephi 16:7
5. Eldest daughter of, married Zoram . . . . 1 Nephi 16:17
6. Sons of, became Lamanites . . . . Alma 17:19
7. Died and was buried in place called Naham . . . . 1 Nephi 16:34
8. Greatly mourned by his daughters . . . . 1 Nephi 16:34
   Note: Ishmael had at least 2 sons and 5 daughters. It appears that the sons
   were married before leaving Jerusalem (1 Ne. 7:6). Ishmael was of the tribe
   of Ephraim, in contrast to Lehi being of Manasseh.

ISHMAEL—before B.C. 80
1. Father of Giddonah . . . . Alma 10:2
2. Descendant of Aminadi . . . . Alma 10:2
3. Descendant of Nephi . . . . Alma 10:2

JACOB, biblical patriarch—1800 B.C.
1. Prophesied concerning a remnant of the seed
   of Joseph as typified by the preservation of a part of
   Joseph's coat . . . . Alma 46:24-26; 3 Nephi 10:17
   Note: This prophecy has not been preserved in the Bible.

JACOB—born between B.C. 599-595
1. Son of Lehi, born in wilderness . . . . 1 Nephi 18:7
2. Grieved by mother's afflictions . . . . 1 Nephi 18:19
3. Blessed by Lehi . . . . 2 Nephi 2:1-30
4. Even in youth, redeemed and beheld Lord's glory . . . . 2 Nephi 2:3-4
5. Accompanied Nephi in departure from Laman and Lemuel . . . . . 2 Nephi 5:6
6. Consecrated a priest by Nephi . . . . 2 Nephi 5:6; Jacob 1:18
7. Exhorted Nephites; cited Isaiah, plan of salvation,
   destiny of promised land . . . . 2 Nephi 6 to 10
8. Eyewitness of angels . . . . 2 Nephi 10:3; Jacob 7:5, 12
9. Eyewitness of the Redeemer . . . . 2 Nephi 11:3
10. Instructed by Nephi concerning keeping the record . . . . Jacob 1:1-8
11. Taught humility and morality to the Nephites . . . . Jacob 2:1-35
12. Related Zenos' parable of olive trees . . . . Jacob 5 and 6
13. Confronted by Sherem, the Anti-Christ . . . . Jacob 7:6-7
14. Confounded Sherem, who fell to the earth . . . . Jacob 7:8-15
15. Began to be old . . . . Jacob 7:26
16. Instructed son Enos to take plates, keep record . . . . Jacob 7:27

17. Bade farewell to the reader .... Jacob 7:27
Note: Jacob is one of the greatest doctrinal preachers of all scripture.

JACOB—about B.C. 64
1. Lamanite military leader in city of Mulek .... Alma 52:20
2. Zoramite .... Alma 52:20
3. Unconquerable spirit .... Alma 52:20
4. Killed in battle with Moroni's army .... Alma 52:35

JACOB—about A.D. 29
1. Leader of apostate secret band among Nephites .... 3 Nephi 7:9
2. Chosen to be a king .... 3 Nephi 7:10
3. Strong opposition against prophets .... 3 Nephi 7:10
4. Flattered the people .... 3 Nephi 7:12
5. Led his band into north regions to recruit strength .... 3 Nephi 7:12-13

JACOM—early Jaredite
1. Son of Jared .... Ether 6:14
2. Declined persuadings of the people to be king .... Ether 6:14

JARED—early Jaredite
1. Left great tower with brother and families .... Ether 1:33
2. Asked brother to pray that language not be confounded ..... Ether 1:34-36
3. Asked brother to inquire as to where Lord would drive them ..... Ether 1:38
4. Traveled with brother and others toward great sea .... Ether 2:1-3
5. Sailed to promised land .... Ether 6:4-13
6. Had four sons: Jacom, Gilgah, Mahah, Orihah .... Ether 6:14
7. Eight daughters .... Ether 6:20
8. Died .... Ether 6:29

JARED, son of Omer—early Jaredite
1. Son of King Omer .... Ether 8:1
2. Begat sons and daughters .... Ether 8:1
3. Drew away one-half of his father's kingdom .... Ether 8:2
4. Captured father by force and took the whole kingdom .... Ether 8:3
5. Was captured by brothers Esrom and Coriantumr, who
   restored kingdom to their father .... Ether 8:5-6
6. Pleaded for life and was spared .... Ether 8:6
7. Exceedingly sorrowful over loss of kingdom .... Ether 8:7
8. Had heart set on glory of the world .... Ether 8:7
9. Had daughter exceeding expert in wicked devices .... Ether 8:8
10. Cooperated with daughter in plan to destroy King Omer .... Ether 8:11
11. Asked Akish to slay Omner as price to marry daughter .... Ether 8:12
12. Became king when Akish and friends drove Omer away .... Ether 9:1-2
13. Gave daughter to be wife of Akish .... Ether 9:4
14. Slain by son-in-law Akish through secret combination .... Ether 9:5-6

JARED, BROTHER OF—early Jaredite (See page 55.)

JAROM—about 500 B.C.
1. Son of Enos .... Jarom 1:1

22

2. Given charge of plates by his father .... Jarom 1:1
3. Kept records and genealogy on small plates .... Jarom 1:1-2
4. Mentioned two sets of plates: large and small .... Jarom 1:14
5. Delivered plates (small) into hands of son Omni .... Jarom 1:15

JEREMIAH, Hebrew Prophet—about 600 B.C.
1. Prophet; testified of coming of Son of God .... Helaman 8:20
2. Testified of destruction of Jerusalem .... Helaman 8:20
3. Put in prison .... 1 Nephi 7:14
4. Writings of, on plates of brass .... 1 Nephi 6:13

JEREMIAH—A.D. 33
1. One of the Twelve Disciples chosen by Jesus .... 3 Nephi 19:4
2. Present also in group .... 3 Nephi 12:1; 28:1-3

JESUS CHRIST—A.D. 1-33
1. To come 600 years after departure of Lehi from Jerusalem ... 1 Nephi 10:4
2. To be born of Mary,
   land of Jerusalem .... 1 Nephi 11:18; Alma 7:10; Mosiah 3:8
3. To redeem people from sins, not in sins .... Alma 11:33-37; Helaman 5:10
4. The Redeemer, Rock, Son of God .... Helaman 5:12
5. The Well-Beloved .... Helaman 5:47
6. The Holy One of Israel .... 2 Nephi 25:29
7. Testified of by many prophets .... Helaman 8:20, 22
8. Is God, and redeemed his servants .... Helaman 8:23
9. Is God of the land .... Ether 2:12
10. Assured Nephi that sign of his birth would occur .... 3 Nephi 1:13-14
11. Explained why is both Father and Son (Mosiah 15:1-5) ...... 3 Nephi 1:14
12. Spake to people during 3 days of darkness (voice only) .... 3 Nephi 9:1-22
13. Spake 2nd time to Nephites .... 3 Nephi 10:1-8
14. Showed himself to Nephites soon after
    ascension to heaven .... 3 Nephi 10:18; 11-12
15. Was introduced by still, small voice of the Father .... 3 Nephi 11:2-7
16. Ascended from heaven to the Nephites, land Bountiful .... 3 Nephi 11:1, 8
17. Clothed in white robe .... 3 Nephi 11:8
18. Invited multitude to one by one feel prints
    of nails and wounds in his body .... 3 Nephi 11:13-15
19. Is God of Israel, and God of whole earth .... 3 Nephi 11:14
20. Called Nephi from multitude—gave
    power to baptize .... 3 Nephi 11:18-21; 21:1
    (See note, end of this section.)
21. Called eleven others, and gave similar power .... 3 Nephi 11:22; 12:1
22. Gave instructions concerning manner of baptism .... 3 Nephi 11:23-28
23. Declared his doctrine concerning faith,
    repentance, baptism .... 3 Nephi 11:31-41
24. Delivered discourse similar to Sermon on Mount .... 3 Nephi 12; 13; 14
25. Giver of Law of Moses .... 3 Nephi 15:4-5
26. Maker of covenants to ancient Israel .... 3 Nephi 15:5
27. The fulfiller of the law .... 3 Nephi 15:4-8
28. Gave commandments to the chosen twelve .... 3 Nephi 15:11-24
29. Stated that Nephites are the sheep of other fold,
    as spoken in John 10:16 .... 3 Nephi 15:16-24

23

30. Declared his intention to visit the lost tribes .... 3 Nephi 16:1-3; 17:4
31. Commanded Nephites to record his instructions .... 3 Nephi 16:4
32. Spoke concerning gathering of Israel, last days,
    Gentiles, quoted Isaiah .... 3 Nephi 16:5-20
33. Commanded multitude to go home and ponder his sayings . 3 Nephi 17:1-3
34. Promised to return on the morrow .... 3 Nephi 17:3; 19:2
35. Declared that lost tribes not lost to the Father .... 3 Nephi 17:4
36. Healed sick, blind, halt, leprous, and maimed .... 3 Nephi 17:5-10
37. Prayed to Father on behalf of Nephites .... 3 Nephi 17:14-20
38. Wept .... 3 Nephi 17:21
39. Blessed little children, one by one .... 3 Nephi 17:21
40. Wept again .... 3 Nephi 17:22
41. Called for bread and wine .... 3 Nephi 18:1-2
42. Brake and blessed the bread .... 3 Nephi 18:3
43. Gave to the disciples to eat—directed them
    to give to multitude .... 3 Nephi 18:3-4
44. Gave instructions concerning sacramental bread .... 3 Nephi 18:5-7
45. Gave wine to disciples to drink—directed them to give also to
    multitude (Note: no mention of blessing on wine.) .... 3 Nephi 18:8-9
46. Gave instructions concerning sacramental wine .... 3 Nephi 18:10-12
47. Instructed concerning prayer—to pray in his name ...... 3 Nephi 18:15-25
48. Gave further instructions concerning who should
    partake of sacrament .... 3 Nephi 18:28-29
49. Condemned disputations .... 3 Nephi 18:34
50. With his hand touched chosen disciples one by one .... 3 Nephi 18:36
51. Gave disciples power to confer Holy Ghost .... 3 Nephi 18:37
52. Enveloped in a cloud, ascended into heaven ...... 3 Nephi 18:38-39; 19:1
53. Returned next day to Nephite disciples and multitude ... 3 Nephi 19:15-16
54. Commanded disciples to kneel and pray .... 3 Nephi 19:17
55. Prayed to Father; asked for Holy Ghost for disciples .... 3 Nephi 19:19-23
56. Smiled upon his disciples .... 3 Nephi 19:25,30
57. Countenance and garments were exceeding
    white and bright .... 3 Nephi 19:25
58. Prayed again to Father; stated that
    disciples were purified .... 3 Nephi 19:27-29
59. Prayed again; things too marvelous to be spoken
    or written by man .... 3 Nephi 19:31-34
60. Declared that Nephites of greater faith than the Jews ...... 3 Nephi 19:35
61. Explained relation of faith to miracles .... 3 Nephi 19:35-36
62. Brake bread and blessed it, and gave to disciples to eat ..... 3 Nephi 20:3
63. Instructed disciples to break bread and
    give to multitude .... 3 Nephi 20:4
64. Gave wine to disciples to drink .... 3 Nephi 20:5
    Note: No mention of wine being blessed. Compare item No. 45.
65. Commanded disciples to give wine to multitude .... 3 Nephi 20:5
66. Had miraculously provided the bread and the wine .... 3 Nephi 20:6-7
67. Gave instructions about purpose of sacramental emblems . 3 Nephi 20:8-9
68. Commended study of the writings of Isaiah .... 3 Nephi 20:11
69. Explained gathering of Israel in latter days .... 3 Nephi 20:12-46
70. Quoted Micah the Hebrew prophet (Micah 4:12) .... 3 Nephi 20:16
71. Spoke concerning the New Jerusalem in this land .... 3 Nephi 20:22
72. Quoted Moses concerning a Great Prophet (Christ) .... 3 Nephi 20:23

73. Declared that Nephites are Israelites and heirs
to covenant of Abraham . . . . 3 Nephi 20:25-27
74. Quoted Isaiah 52, about future redemption of Israel . . . . . 3 Nephi 20:32-46
75. More about Israel, latter days, Gentiles, Isaiah . . . . 3 Nephi 21:1-29
76. Quoted Isaiah 54 . . . . 3 Nephi 22:1-17
77. Again commanded people to study
and search Isaiah's writings . . . . 3 Nephi 23:1-3
78. Commanded the study and search of the prophets . . . . 3 Nephi 23:5
79. Commanded that his own words be written . . . . 3 Nephi 23:4, 14
80. Expounded all scriptures to the people . . . . 3 Nephi 23:6, 14
81. Pointed out omissions in Nephite record concerning prophecies of
Samuel the Lamanite; commanded these be written . . . . . . 3 Nephi 23:6-13
82. Quoted Malachi 3, 4; commanded these be written in
Nephite record for use in future generations . . . . 3 Nephi 24-25; 26:2
83. Expounded all things, great and small . . . . 3 Nephi 26:1
84. Expounded all things from beginning to end . . . . 3 Nephi 26:3-4
85. Taught more than 100 times as much as is
written of him in 3 Nephi . . . . 3 Nephi 26:6
86. Taught the people for three days . . . . 3 Nephi 26:13
87. Showed himself oft to the multitude . . . . 3 Nephi 26:13
88. Often broke bread and gave to multitude . . . . 3 Nephi 26:13
89. Blessed little children; loosing their tongues
to speak great and marvelous things . . . . 3 Nephi 26:14, 16
90. Did all manner of healing; raised one from the dead . . . . 3 Nephi 26:15
91. Showed himself to disciples; named his church . . . . 3 Nephi 27:1-11
92. Gave instructions concerning gospel; repentance . . . . . . 3 Nephi 27:12-19
93. Discussed sanctification . . . . 3 Nephi 27:20
94. Declared judgment to be out of the books . . . . 3 Nephi 27:24-26
95. Declared salvation for that generation . . . . 3 Nephi 27:30-31
96. Predicted falling away and apostasy in 4th generation . . . . . . 3 Nephi 27:32
97. Granted each disciple his individual desire . . . . 3 Nephi 28:1-2
98. Promised nine that they would
be saved in heaven at death . . . . 3 Nephi 28:2-3
99. Read thoughts of three disciples who durst not speak . . . . . 3 Nephi 28:4-6
100. Compared the three to John the Beloved . . . . 3 Nephi 28:6
101. Promised power over death to the three . . . . 3 Nephi 28:7-9
102. Promised the three they could remain on earth to
behold all the doings of the Father among men until
second coming . . . . 3 Nephi 28:7
103. Promised the three they would sit down in
kingdom of heaven . . . . 3 Nephi 28:10
104. Touched the nine with his finger . . . . 3 Nephi 28:12
105. Departed from the disciples . . . . 3 Nephi 28:12

*Note: Item No. 20. The baptism spoken of in 3 Nephi 11:18-21 was un-
doubtedly to be a second baptism for most, if not all, of the people. Their
former baptism was under the law. Although this was valid, a new dispensation was being ushered in, which required a new baptism. These people
were in a unique situation, that of living through the end of one dispensation
into another. Compare D&C 22.*

JOHN, Jewish Apostle—about A.D. 1-100
1. One of the twelve apostles of the Lamb . . . . 1 Nephi 14:20, 27

25

2. Ordained to write concerning end of the world ....1 Nephi 14:22, 25
3. Writings of, are just and true ....1 Nephi 14:23
4. Writings of, to be in record of the Jews ....1 Nephi 14:23
5. Wrote of many things Nephi saw in vision ....1 Nephi 14:24
6. With Jesus among the Jews ....3 Nephi 28:6
7. Never to taste of death ....3 Nephi 28:6-9
8. Record of, to be revealed in last days ....Ether 4:16

JONAS—about 33 A.D.
1. One of Twelve Disciples chosen by Jesus .... 3 Nephi 19:4
2. Son of Nephi (also a disciple) .... 3 Nephi 19:4
3. Present with the others on occasion .... 3 Nephi 12:1; 28:3

JONAS—about 33 A.D.
1. One of Twelve Disciples chosen by Jesus ....3 Nephi 19:4
2. Present with others on occasion ....3 Nephi 12:1; 28:3

JONEAM—about A.D. 385
1. Nephite military leader with 10,000 men at Cumorah .... Mormon 6:14
2. Slain in battle .... Mormon 6:14

JOSEPH, youngest son of Lehi—born shortly after B.C. 600
1. Born in the wilderness .... 1 Nephi 18:7
2. Grieved by his mother's afflictions .... 1 Nephi 18:19
3. Blessed by Lehi .... 2 Nephi 3:1-25
4. Promised that his seed would never be
   completely destroyed .... 2 Nephi 3:3, 23
5. Journeyed with Nephi into wilderness away from
   Laman and Lemuel (in promised land) .... 2 Nephi 5:6
6. Consecrated a priest by Nephi .... Jacob 1:18; 2 Nephi 5:26

JOSEPH, Hebrew patriarch, son of Jacob—about B.C. 1700
1. Ancestor of Nephites and Lamanites .... 1 Nephi 5:14; 6:2
                          2 Nephi 3:4; Alma 10:3; 46:24; 3 Nephi 15:12
2. Ancestor to Laban, keeper of the plates of brass .... 1 Nephi 5:16
3. Truly saw day of Nephites (by vision and prophecy) .... 2 Nephi 3:5
4. Carried captive into Egypt .... 2 Nephi 3:4, 4:1
                          1 Nephi 5:14; Alma 10:3
5. Obtained promise from Lord that his posterity would
   be a righteous branch of Israel .... 2 Nephi 3:5
6. Testified of latter-day, choice seer named Joseph .... 2 Nephi 3:6, 15
7. Testified of Moses to lead Israel from Egypt .... 2 Nephi 3:9, 10, 16, 17
8. Prophesied concerning all his seed; Nephites
   and future generations .... 2 Nephi 4:2
9. Great covenants made to .... 2 Nephi 3:4
10. Not many greater prophecies than those of Joseph .... 2 Nephi 4:2
11. Writing and prophecies of, upon plates of brass .... 2 Nephi 4:2
12. Was promised that his seed should never perish
    from earth .... 2 Nephi 25:21
13. Brought his father into Egypt .... Ether 13:7
14. Died in Egypt .... Ether 13:7
15. Remnant of coat preserved .... Alma 46:24

26

JOSH—about A.D. 385
1. Nephite military leader with 10,000 men at Cumorah .... Mormon 6:14
2. Slain in battle .... Mormon 6:14

KIB—early Jaredite
1. Son of Orihah's old age .... Ether 1:32; 7:3
2. Succeeded his father as Jaredite king .... Ether 7:3
3. Overthrown by his son Corihor; dwelt in captivity .... Ether 7:4-5
4. In old age, and in captivity, begat son Shule .... Ether 7:7
5. Restored to the kingdom by efforts of son Shule .... Ether 7:9
6. Conferred the kingdom on Shule .... Ether 7:10

KIM—middle Jaredite
1. Son of King Morianton .... Ether 1:22; 10:13
2. Succeeded his father as king .... Ether 10:13
3. Reigned eight years before his father died .... Ether 10:13
4. Did not do right in sight of God .... Ether 10:13
5. Brought into captivity by rebellion of his brother .... Ether 10:14
6. Remained in captivity all the remainder of days .... Ether 10:14
7. Begat sons and daughters .... Ether 10:14
8. In old age begat Levi .... Ether 10:14
9. Died .... Ether 10:14

KIMNOR—early Jaredite
1. Father of Akish .... Ether 8:10

KISH—middle Jaredite
1. Son of King Corom .... Ether 10:17; 1:19
2. Succeeded his father as king .... Ether 10:17
3. Passed away .... Ether 10:18
4. Succeeded by son Lib as king .... Ether 10:18; 1:18

KISHKUMEN—about B.C. 50
1. Murdered chief judge, Pahoran II, upon the judgment seat .... Helaman 1:9
2. Avoided detection because of disguise and
   speedy escape .... Helaman 1:11-12
3. Made covenant with certain friends that they would
   not reveal his identity as murderer of Pahoran II .... Helaman 1:11; 2:3
4. Sought the life of Helaman .... Helaman 2:3
5. Unwittingly gave knowledge of murder plot to
   one of Helaman's servants .... Helaman 2:6-8
6. Was stabbed in heart (died without groan) by
   servant of Helaman .... Helaman 2:9

KORIHOR—about B.C. 74
1. Anti-Christ in Zarahemla .... Alma 30:6-12
2. Taught that there would be no Christ .... Alma 30:12
3. Journeyed to Jershon to teach people of Ammon .... Alma 30:19
4. Had little success .... Alma 30:21
5. Preached in land Gideon; denied all prophecy, revelation ... Alma 30:21-28
6. Bound; sent to Zarahemla to be judged of Alma .... Alma 30:29

7. Blasphemed great swelling words before Alma . . . . Alma 30:30-31
8. Rebuked by Alma, desired a sign and was stricken . . . . Alma 30:32-50
9. Confessed sin; became house-to-house beggar for food . . . . Alma 30:52-58
10. Run upon and trodden down until dead . . . . Alma 30:59
11. Example that the devil does not support his own . . . . Alma 30:60

KUMEN—about A.D. 33
1. One of Twelve Disciples chosen by Jesus . . . . 3 Nephi 19:4
2. Also present on occasion with others . . . . 3 Nephi 12:1; 28:1-3

KUMENONHI—about A.D. 33
1. One of the Twelve Disciples chosen by Jesus . . . . 3 Nephi 19:4
2. Also present on occasion with others . . . . 3 Nephi 12:1; 28:1-3

LABAN—about B.C. 600
1. Lived in Jerusalem, had record of the Jews . . . . 1 Nephi 3:2-3
2. Refused to give record of Jews (brass plates) to Laman . . . . 1 Nephi 3:13
3. Sought to slay Laman . . . . 1 Nephi 3:13
4. Refused to sell the record of the Jews to Nephi
   and brethren . . . . 1 Nephi 3:24
5. Lusted after Nephi's gold; sent servants to slay
   Nephi and brethren . . . . 1 Nephi 3:25
6. Obtained Nephi's gold and wealth . . . . 1 Nephi 3:26
7. Able to command and even slay fifty; a mighty man . . . . 1 Nephi 3:31
8. Drunken by night . . . . 1 Nephi 4:5-8
9. Possessed exceeding fine sword . . . . 1 Nephi 4:9
10. Slain with own sword by Nephi . . . . 1 Nephi 4:18-19
11. Had servant and treasury . . . . 1 Nephi 4:20
12. Descendant of Joseph . . . . 1 Nephi 5:16
13. He and his fathers had kept the records · . . . . 1 Nephi 5:16

LACHONEUS, the elder—about A.D. 26 (Was judge at time of Christ's birth)
1. Chief judge and governor of Nephites . . . . 3 Nephi 1:1
2. Received epistle from Giddianhi, leader of robbers,
   calling for complete Nephite surrender . . . . 3 Nephi 3:1-10
3. Astonished at boldness of Giddianhi . . . . 3 Nephi 3:11
4. A just man—not frightened by a robber . . . . 3 Nephi 3:12
5. Sought to God for help . . . . 3 Nephi 3:12
6. Built fortifications and other preparations for defense . . . . . . 3 Nephi 3:12-14
7. Preached and prophesied mightily . . . . 3 Nephi 3:16, 19
8. Appointed chief captains over armies as defense
   against robbers . . . . 3 Nephi 3:17
9. Gathered many thousands into land southward . . . . 3 Nephi 3:22-24
10. Given just credit for establishing peace among Nephites . . . . . . 3 Nephi 6:6
11. Was succeeded by son Lachoneus . . . . 3 Nephi 6:19

LACHONEUS, the younger—about A.D. 26
1. Son of Lachoneus, the chief judge . . . . 3 Nephi 6:19
2. Appointed chief judge to succeed his father (A.D. 26) . . . . 3 Nephi 6:19
3. Murdered (?) by self-seeking and ambitious men . . . . 3 Nephi 7:1

LAMAH—about A.D. 385
1. Nephite military leader with 10,000 at Cumorah .... Mormon 6:14
2. Slain in battle .... Mormon 6:14

LAMAN—about B.C. 600
1. Eldest son of Lehi .... 1 Nephi 2:5; 2:12; Alma 56:3
2. Murmured against Lehi, calling him visionary man, etc. ..... 1 Nephi 2:11-12
3. Like unto the Jews who sought to kill Lehi .... 1 Nephi 2:13
4. Left Jerusalem with Lehi and family .... 1 Nephi 2:4-5
5. Returned to Jerusalem to obtain brass plates from Laban ...... 1 Nephi 3:9
6. Fled from Laban's house to save life .... 1 Nephi 3:11-14
7. Desired to return to Lehi in wilderness without plates .... 1 Nephi 3:14
8. Persuaded by Nephi to try again to get plates .... 1 Nephi 3:15-21
9. Became angry with Nephi and smote him with a rod .... 1 Nephi 3:28
10. Rebuked by an angel .... 1 Nephi 3:29; 7:10
11. Commanded by angel to return for the plates .... 1 Nephi 3:29
12. Murmured again, doubting words of the angel .... 1 Nephi 3:31
13. Returned to Lehi, after Nephi secured the plates .... 1 Nephi 4:38
14. Returned to Jerusalem second time to persuade
    Ishmael and family to join them in wilderness .... 1 Nephi 7:2-5
15. Rebelled with Lemuel and 2 daughters of Ishmael,
    against Lehi and Nephi .... 1 Nephi 7:6-7
16. With Lemuel, bound Nephi with cords, desiring his death ..... 1 Nephi 7:16
17. Witnessed power of God in release of Nephi's bonds ...... 1 Nephi 7:17-18
18. Again sought to seize Nephi in anger .... 1 Nephi 7:19
19. Repented and begged Nephi's forgiveness .... 1 Nephi 7:20
20. Failed to inquire of the Lord for information .... 1 Nephi 15:2-3
21. Denied that the Lord makes known meaning
    of prophecies .... 1 Nephi 15:8-9
22. Questioned Nephi concerning meaning
    of Lehi's dream .... 1 Nephi 15:21-31
23. Murmured at Nephi; complained he was too strict .... 1 Nephi 16:1-4
24. Humbled himself as result of Nephi's preaching, exhortation .. 1 Nephi 16:5
25. Married one of daughters of Ishmael .... 1 Nephi 16:7
26. Angered at Nephi because he (Nephi) broke bow .... 1 Nephi 16:18
27. Murmured against the Lord because of afflictions .... 1 Nephi 16:19-20
28. Hardened heart against the Lord .... 1 Nephi 16:22
29. Humbled himself after obtaining food from Nephi .... 1 Nephi 16:32
30. Proposed to kill Lehi and Nephi .... 1 Nephi 16:37
31. Stirred up hearts of brethren against Nephi .... 1 Nephi 16:38
32. Called Nephi a liar and deceiver .... 1 Nephi 16:38
33. Was severely chastened by voice of the Lord .... 1 Nephi 16:39
34. Humbled himself and repented of sins .... 1 Nephi 16:39
35. Lived eight years in wilderness with brethren and family ...... 1 Nephi 17:4
36. Called Nephi a fool for building a ship .... 1 Nephi 17:17
37. Unwilling to labor on building of the ship .... 1 Nephi 17:18
38. Rejoiced over Nephi's sorrow; said he lacked judgment ..... 1 Nephi 17:19
39. Murmured against Lehi and Nephi .... 1 Nephi 17:20
40. Falsely declared that the Jews were righteous .... 1 Nephi 17:22
41. Described by Nephi as murderous at heart .... 1 Nephi 17:44
42. Attempted to throw Nephi into the depths of the sea .... 1 Nephi 17:48
43. Shaken and shocked by the power of God .... 1 Nephi 17:48-54

29

44. Fell at Nephi's feet to worship him .... 1 Nephi 17:55
45. Repented again and began to help Nephi build ship .... 1 Nephi 18:1
46. Humbled himself before the Lord .... 1 Nephi 18:4
47. Entered ship with the group bound for promised land .... 1 Nephi 18:6
48. Made merry and used rudeness of speech aboard ship .... 1 Nephi 18:9
49. Angered at Nephi; accused him of seeking power .... 1 Nephi 18:10
50. With Lemuel, bound Nephi with cords .... 1 Nephi 18:11
51. Frightened by storm at sea .... 1 Nephi 18:13-15
52. Repented; released Nephi from bonds .... 1 Nephi 18:15
53. Breathed out threatenings against all who
    befriended Nephi .... 1 Nephi 18:17
54. Hardened against all influence except power of God .... 1 Nephi 18:20
55. Questioned Nephi concerning his teachings .... 1 Nephi 22:1
56. Was exhorted, blessed, and warned by Lehi .... 2 Nephi 1:28-29
57. Angered at Nephi soon after Lehi's death .... 2 Nephi 4:13
58. Sought with others to slay Nephi .... 2 Nephi 5:2-4
59. Not all murmurings are recorded .... 2 Nephi 5:4
60. Mark placed upon, for unrighteousness .... Alma 3:7; 2 Nephi 5:21

LAMAN, Lamanite king—About B.C. 250
1. Lamanite king, land Lehi-Nephi during same time
   Mosiah was king in Zarahemla .... Mosiah 9:10-13
2. Made covenant with Zeniff giving him (Zeniff)
   possession of city Lehi-Nephi .... Mosiah 9:6-9
3. Broke covenant; made war upon people of Zeniff .... Mosiah 9:10-13
4. Died approximately B.C. 178 .... Mosiah 10:6
5. Succeeded in kingship by son Laman .... Mosiah 24:3

LAMAN, Lamanite king—about B.C. 178
1. King of Lamanites in time of Alma (the elder) .... Mosaih 24:3
2. Succeeded and named after his father .... Mosiah 24:3
3. King over numerous people .... Mosiah 24:3
4. Stirred up his people against Zeniff's people .... Mosiah 10:6

LAMAN—about B.C. 63
1. A man in Moroni's army .... Alma 55:4-5
2. Sought out by Moroni for special duty .... Alma 55:4-5
3. Former servant of Lamanite king who had been slain
   by Amalickiah .... Alma 55:5
4. Went with small number of men to the guards over
   the Nephites in city Gid .... Alma 55:6-7
5. As strategy, took wine to Lamanite guards .... Alma 55:8
6. Received with joy by the Lamanite guards .... Alma 55:8-9
7. Enticed guards to consume much wine .... Alma 55:10-14
8. Returned with his men to report to Moroni
   that guards were drunken .... Alma 55:15

LAMONI—about B.C. 90
1. Descendant of Ishmael .... Alma 17:21
2. King of Lamanites in land of Ishmael .... Alma 17:21
3. Desired Ammon, son of Mosiah, to marry his daughter .... Alme 17:24
4. Mistook Ammon for the Great Spirit .... Alma 17:2-4, 11

30

5. Son of Lamanite king (name not given) who was
   king over all the land .... Alma 18:9
6. Afraid of Ammon and durst not speak .... Alma 18:11-15
7. Believed all the words of Ammon .... Alma 18:40
8. Being overcome by the Spirit, fell as though dead .... Alma 18:42-43
9. Arose and taught Ammon's words to his people .... Alma 19:30-31
10. Went to land Middoni with Ammon to free
    Ammon's brethren from prison .... Alma 20:4, 28
11. Friend of Antiomno, king of land of Middoni .... Alma 20:4
12. Met father, who opposed his friendship with Ammon .... Alma 20:8-26
13. Given land Ishmael as own by father, who was
    supreme Lamanite king .... Alma 20:26
14. Built synagogues in his land; gave freedom of worship ...... Alma 21:18-22

LEHI—B.C. 600

1. Born in Jerusalem .... 1 Nephi 1:4
2. Saw vision of pillar of fire; throne of God .... 1 Nephi 1:6-10; Alma 36:22
3. Testified to Jews in Jerusalem of their wickedness .... 1 Nephi 1:18
4. Prophesied of destruction of Jerusalem .... 1 Nephi 1:18
5. Life of, sought by Jews .... 1 Nephi 1:20
6. Commanded of Lord in dream to depart with family
   into desert. Compare 3 Nephi 4:11; 5:15; 5:20 .... 1 Nephi 2:1-3
7. Traveled near Red Sea for three days .... 1 Nephi 2:6
8. Built altar of stone; gave names to valley and river .... 1 Nephi 2:7-10
9. Dwelt in a tent in the wilderness .... 1 Nephi 2:15
10. Received command from Lord to send sons back
    to Jerusalem to obtain plates of brass from Laban .... 1 Nephi 2:2-4
11. Rejoiced at sons' return to tent in wilderness .... 1 Nephi 5:1-7
12. Affirmed to Sariah that he was a visionary man .... 1 Nephi 5:4
13. Searched the plates of brass diligently .... 1 Nephi 5:10
14. A descendant of Joseph .... Alma 10:3; 1 Nephi 5:14
15. Prophesied that the brass plates would be
    preserved and not be dimmed by time .... 1 Nephi 5:17-20
16. Kept record of genealogies of his father .... 1 Nephi 6:1
17. Received command from Lord that his sons should again
    return to Jerusalem to bring Ishmael and family to Lehi .... 1 Nephi 7:1-3
18. Gathered all kinds of seeds and fruits .... 1 Nephi 8:1
19. Had dream concerning Laman, Lemuel, Sam, Nephi .... 1 Nephi 8:2-4
20. Exhorted Laman, Lemuel to faithfulness .... 1 Nephi 8:36-38
21. Explained concerning Jews, Jerusalem and coming of
    Messiah in 600 years .... 1 Nephi 10:2-4
22. Predicted birth, baptism, death, resurrection of Messiah ... 1 Nephi 10:7-11
23. Spoke of scattering and gathering of Israel .... 1 Nephi 10:12-14
24. Found brass ball, director (Liahona) at tent door . 1 Nephi 16:10; Alma 37:38
25. Murmured against Lord for lack of food .... 1 Nephi 16:20
26. Repented after chastening from the Lord .... 1 Nephi 16:25
27. Commanded of Lord to enter ship constructed by Nephi ...... 1 Nephi 18:5
28. Begat two sons while in wilderness (Jacob and Joseph) ...... 1 Nephi 18:7
29. Said many things to Laman, Lemuel because of their
    hardness of heart and hatred for Nephi .... 1 Nephi 18:17
30. Nearly died of grief and sorrow because of
    wickedness of Laman, Lemuel .... 1 Nephi 18:18

LEHI—about B.C. 80

LEHI—about B.C. 74

LEHI, son of Helaman—about B.C. 45

8. Cast into prison by Lamanites (same prison into
   which Ammon had been cast) .... Helaman 5:21
9. Many days without food .... Helaman 5:22
10. Circled about by fire; protected from Lamanites .... Helaman 5:23-24
11. Preserved (with Nephi) within cloud of darkness and a voice
    above the cloud declared them to be servants of God ..... Helaman 5:28-34
12. Face shone as an angel's; appeared to converse
    with heavenly being .... Helaman 5:35-39
13. Ministered unto by angels .... Helaman 5:38-48
14. Went into land northward to preach .... Helaman 6:6
15. Not one whit behind Nephi in righteousness .... Helaman 11:19
16. Had many revelations daily .... Helaman 11:23

LEHONTI—about B.C. 50
1. Leader of Lamanite group not wanting war .... Alma 47:10
2. Refused to have conference with Amalickiah .... Alma 47:1-12
3. Entered into agreement with Amalickiah to conquer
   Amalickiah's army and to make Amalickiah second man,
   under himself .... Alma 47:13-17
4. Poisoned by Amalickiah's servant .... Alma 47:17-19

LEMUEL—about B.C. 600
1. Second son of Lehi .... 1 Nephi 2:5
Note: Entries for Lemuel and Laman are so identical that it seemed un-
necessary to list the material twice. Please see the biography of Laman, son
of Lehi. Entries therein are applicable to Lemuel.

LEVI—middle Jaredite
1. Son of Kim .... Ether 10:14; 1:21
2. Begotten when father was old man .... Ether 10:14
3. Served in captivity 42 years after death of father .... Ether 10:15
4. Rebelled against king and obtained kingdom for himself .... Ether 10:15
5. Did right in sight of the Lord .... Ether 10:16
6. Lived to good old age .... Ether 10:16
7. Begat sons and daughters .... Ether 10:16
8. Begat Corom and anointed him king .... Ether 10:16

LIB—middle Jaredite
1. Son of King Kish .... Ether 10:18; 1:18
2. Succeeded his father as king .... Ether 10:18
3. Was good king .... Ether 10:19
4. Became great hunter .... Ether 10:19
5. Reigned over a prosperous and blessed people .... Ether 10:20-28
6. Lived many years .... Ether 10:29
7. Begat sons and daughters .... Ether 10:29
8. Begat Hearthom .... Ether 10:29
9. Was succeeded as king by Hearthom .... Ether 10:29

LIB—late Jaredite
1. Man of secret combination .... Ether 14:10
2. Obtained kingdom of the Jaredites .... Ether 14:10
3. Man of greater stature than any other Jaredite of the time ...... Ether 14:10

33

4. Fought with Coriantumr; wounded Coriantumr on arm .... Ether 14:12
5. Fled from Coriantumr's army .... Ether 14:12
6. Renewed battle and overcame Coriantumr's armies .... Ether 14:14
7. Slain by Coriantumr on plains of Agosh .... Ether 14:16
8. Succeeded by his brother Shiz .... Ether 14:17

LIMHAH—about 385 A.D.
1. Nephite military leader with 10,000 men at Cumorah .... Mormon 6:14
2. Slain in battle .... Mormon 6:14

LIMHER—about B.C. 87
1. One of 4 spies sent by Alma to observe Amlicites .... Alma 2:21-22
2. Returned with word that Amlicites and Lamanites
   were coming to battle .... Alma 2:23-26
3. See Zeram, Amnor, Manti

LIMHI—about B.C. 120
1. Appointed king of people in land Nephi by
   popular choice (after Noah) .... Mosiah 7:8-9; 19:26
2. Son of King Noah, who was son of Zeniff .... Mosiah 7:9
3. Captured Ammon and friends; questioned them .... Mosiah 7:7-11
4. Released Ammon and friends when learned
   they were from Zarahemla .... Mosiah 7:16
5. Gave Ammon some plates containing record of
   people from time they left Zarahemla .... Mosiah 8:5
6. Praised Lord when learned that Mosiah could translate
   the twenty-four gold plates which he (Limhi) had .... Mosiah 8:19-21
7. A just man .... Mosiah 19:17
8. Taken captive by Lamanites at time that Gideon
   was about to slay Noah .... Mosiah 19:7-16
9. Made oath with Lamanites to pay tribute of
   one-half of possessions .... Mosiah 19:26
10. Established peace among his people .... Mosiah 19:27
11. Fought with Lamanites in defense of his people .... Mosiah 20:6-11
12. Sent men from land Nephi in search of Zarahemla .... Mosiah 21:35
13. Would have been baptized but none in land had
    authority (didn't know where Alma was) .... Mosiah 21:32-36
14. Cooperated with Gideon on plan to free
    people from Lamanites .... Mosiah 22:9
15. After freeing people from Lamanites, united them with
    people of Mosiah in land Zarahemla .... Mosiah 22:10-13
16. Baptized by Alma .... Mosiah 25:17-18

LURAM—about A.D. 385
1. Nephite soldier slain in last struggle of Nephites .... Moroni 9:2

MAHAH—early Jaredite
1. Son of Jared .... Ether 6:14
2. Declined the persuadings of the people to become king .... Ether 6:27

MALACHI, Hebrew prophet—about B.C. 400
1. Quotations from, cited by Jesus .... 3 Nephi 24, 25

34

MANTI—about B.C. 87
1. One of four spies sent by Alma to observe Amlicites .... Alma 2:21-22
2. Returned with word that Amlicites and Lamanites
   were coming to battle .... Alma 2:23-26

MARY, mother of Jesus—prophetic reference only
1. Beautiful, fair, and white virgin .... 1 Nephi 11:13-15
2. Mother of the Son of God according to the flesh.
   Compare Alma 7:10 .... 1 Nephi 11:18; Mosiah 3:8
3. Lived at Nazareth .... 1 Nephi 11:13

MATHONI—about A.D. 33
1. One of Twelve Disciples chosen by Jesus .... 3 Nephi 19:4
2. Brother of Mathonihah (?) .... 3 Nephi 19:4
3. Present on occasion with others .... 3 Nephi 12:1; 28:3

MATHONIHAH—about A.D. 33
1. One of Twelve Disciples chosen by Jesus .... 3 Nephi 19:4
2. Brother of Mathoni (?) .... 3 Nephi 19:4
3. Present on occasion with others .... 3 Nephi 12:1; 28:3

MORIANTON—about B.C. 67
1. Leader of rebellion among Nephites .... Alma 50:28
2. Afraid to fight Moroni's army .... Alma 50:28
3. Planned to possess land northward; land of many lakes .... Alma 50:29
4. Man of much passion; beat his servant girl .... Alma 50:30
5. Led his armies into northland .... Alma 50:35
6. Slain by Teancum .... Alma 50:35; 51:29

MORIANTON—middle Jaredite
1. Descendant of Riplakish .... Ether 10:9; 1:23
2. Gathered army; established himself as Jaredite king .... Ether 10:9
3. Eased tax burden; became popular in eyes of people .... Ether 10:10
4. Did justice to people but not to himself .... Ether 10:11
5. Committed many whoredoms .... Ether 10:11
6. Built many cities .... Ether 10:12
7. Was king at a prosperous time .... Ether 10:12
8. Lived to extremely old age .... Ether 10:13
9. Begat Kim in old age .... Ether 10:13
10. Lived eight years after Kim succeeded him as king .... Ether 10:13

MORMON—about 300 A.D.
1. Father of Mormon, abridger of Nephite records .... Mormon 1:5; 8:13
2. Moved southward to land Zarahemla .... Mormon 1:6

MORMON—about A.D. 310-385
1. Named after the place and land of Mormon .... 3 Nephi 5:12
2. A disciple of Jesus Christ .... 3 Nephi 5:13
3. Called to declare the word of God .... 3 Nephi 5:13
4. Made a small record of the account kept by Nephites
   from time that Lehi left Jerusalem .... 3 Nephi 5:14-19
5. Record of, was just and true .... 3 Nephi 5:18

6. Unable to write many things because of
   difficulty of language .... 3 Nephi 5:18
7. Pure descendant of Lehi .... 3 Nephi 5:20
8. Descendant of Nephi .... Mormon 1:5; 8:13
9. Restrained by the Lord from writing more .... 3 Nephi 26:11
10. Wrote the things the Lord commanded .... 3 Nephi 26:12
11. Forbidden by Lord to write names of the Three Nephites ..... 3 Nephi 28:25
12. Was ministered unto by the Three Nephite disciples .... 3 Nephi 28:26
13. Inquired of Lord concerning status of Three Nephites .... 3 Nephi 28:36-37
14. Learned of translated status of Three Nephites .... 3 Nephi 28:37-40
15. Warned readers to repent, accept miracles, believe gospel .. 3 Nephi 29:1-9
16. Upheld the Jews, as heirs to the covenant of Israel .... 3 Nephi 29:8
17. Called Gentiles to repentance .... 3 Nephi 30:1-2
18. Made record of things he saw and heard; called it
    the book of Mormon .... Mormon 1:1
19. Received instructions from prophet Ammaron .... Mormon 1:2
20. Was sober child; quick to observe .... Mormon 1:2, 15
21. Was ten years of age in year A.D. 320. (See 4 Nephi 48) .... Mormon 1:2
22. Instructed by Ammaron to obtain sacred records from
    hill Shim when about age 24 (about 334 A.D.) .... Mormon 1:3
23. Son of Mormon .... Mormon 1:5; 8:13
24. Taken by father to Zarahemla, at age 11 .... Mormon 1:6
25. When age 15 was visited by the Lord; tasted
    goodness of Jesus .... Mormon 1:15
26. Attempted to preach to Nephites; restrained by the Lord ...... Mormon 1:16
27. Large in stature, although quite young .... Mormon 2:1
28. Appointed military leader, Nephite armies; age 15 .... Mormon 2:1
29. Led Nephite armies to battle; age 16 .... Mormon 2:2
30. Defeated Lamanite army of superior numbers .... Mormon 2:9
31. Witnessed wickedness and destruction of many Nephites .. Mormon 2:12-18
32. Obtained sacred record from hill Shim .... Mormon 2:17; 4:23
33. Made 2 records: full account on plates of Nephi;
    partial account on own plates .... Mormon 2:18
34. Sorrowed because of wickedness and destruction
    of Nephites .... Mormon 2:19
35. Encouraged and aroused the Nephites to fight boldly
    against Lamanites, in defense of home, family .... Mormon 2:23-24
36. With army of 30,000, defeated Lamanite army of 50,000 ...... Mormon 2:25
37. Enacted treaty with Lamanites for division of land.
    Nephites possessed land north of narrow passage; Lamanites
    possessed land south of narrow passage .... Mormon 2:28-29
38. Spent ten years preparing people, cities, for war .... Mormon 3:1
39. Preached faith, repentance, baptism to Nephites: no avail ... Mormon 3:2-3
40. Received epistle from Lamanite king stating the
    Lamanites were coming to battle Nephites .... Mormon 3:4
41. Gathered his people near narrow pass in land Desolation .... Mormon 3:5-6
42. With Nephite army, defeated Lamanites over period
    of two years .... Mormon 3:7-8
43. Refused to continue as Nephite leader due to their
    gross wickedness .... Mormon 3:11, 16
44. Had led, loved Nephites; thrice had delivered
    them from Lamanites .... Mormon 3:12-13

45. Could not hope for preservation of such wicked Nephites .. Mormon 3:12-15
46. Stood as idle witness and example of righteousness .... Mormon 3:16
47. Wrote unto Gentiles, Israel of latter days, to repent .... Mormon 3:17-22
48. Witnessed extreme wickedness of Nephites .... Mormon 4:12
49. Witnessed extreme bloodshed and carnage of Nephites ... Mormon 4:11-15
50. Relented, again became Nephite military leader .... Mormon 5:1
51. Witnessed additional scenes of carnage; bloodshed .... Mormon 5:2-9
52. Made abridgment, purposely not giving full account
    of the affairs among his people .... Mormon 5:9
53. Wrote for benefit of Israel, Gentiles in latter days .... Mormon 5:10-24
54. Prophesied of Lamanite, Gentile on this land in last days .. Mormon 5:14-24
55. Wrote epistle to Lamanite king, inviting him to
    battle in land of Cumorah .... Mormon 6:2
56. Gathered Nephites at Cumorah for battle, A.D. 385 .... Mormon 6:4-5
57. Began to be old .... Mormon 6:6
58. Knew that Cumorah battle would be final .... Mormon 6:6
59. Hid records in Hill Cumorah to protect them from Lamanites ... Mormon 6:6
60. Witnessed destruction of 230,000 Nephites at Cumorah ... Mormon 6:11-14
61. Personally led 10,000 soldiers into fatal battle at Cumorah .... Mormon 6:11
62. Among 24 survivors at Cumorah, while 230,000 slain .... Mormon 6:11
63. Killed by the Lamanites at Cumorah, about A.D. 385 .... Mormon 8:3, 5
64. Explained purpose and intent of the sacred records ..... Mormon 8:5; 7:1-9
65. Epistle about faith, hope, charity .... Mormon 7:1-48
66. Epistle to Moroni concerning nonbaptism of little children ... Mormon 8:1-30
67. Epistle to Moroni concerning atrocities of Lamanites
    and Nephites .... Mormon 9:1-26

MORON—late Jaredite
1. Son of Ethem .... Ether 11:14; 1:8
2. Succeeded Ethem as king .... Ether 11:14
3. Wicked king .... Ether 11:14
4. Lost one-half of kingdom for many years to mighty
   man of secret combination .... Ether 11:15
5. After many years overthrew the mighty man
   and regained kingdom .... Ether 11:16
6. Brought into captivity again by second mighty man,
   a descendant of brother of Jared .... Ether 11:17-18
7. Begat Coriantor .... Ether 11:18; 1:7
8. Dwelt in captivity all the remainder of his days .... Ether 11:18

MORONI—about B.C. 100
1. Chief commander of Nephite armies .... Alma 43:16-17; 46:11
2. Armed people with swords, cimeters, weapons of war .... Alma 43:18
3. Prepared people with armor, thick clothing, shields .... Alma 43:19
4. Sent spies to watch Lamanite camp .... Alma 43:23
5. Asked Alma to inquire of Lord concerning
   where to fight Lamanites .... Alma 43:23
6. Encircled Lamanites by strategem near River
   Sidon and land Manti .... Alma 43:25-53
7. Commanded his men not to slay Lamanites .... Alma 43:54
8. Offered Lamanites freedom on condition of no more war .... Alma 44:17

MORONI—about A.D. 350-420

1. Son of Mormon .... Mormon 6:11-12; 8:13
2. Led 10,000 people into fatal battle at Cumorah .... Mormon 6:12
3. Among 24 survivors .... Mormon 6:11
4. Finished record of Mormon .... Mormon 8:1
5. Remained alone to witness complete Nephite destruction .... Mormon 8:3-5
6. Without friends or kinsfolk .... Mormon 8:5-6
7. Visited by three Nephite disciples .... Mormon 8:11
8. If possible, would make all things known .... Mormon 8:12
9. Commends acceptance of the Nephite record .... Mormon 8:12-17
10. Commends the writings of Isaiah .... Mormon 8:23
11. Prophesied of latter-day conditions .... Mormon 8:25-41
12. Testified of worth of Christ; directed to unbelievers .... Mormon 9:1-31
13. Lord had shown doings of men in last days .... Mormon 9:35
14. Wrote in characters called "reformed Egyptian" .... Mormon 9:32
15. Gave abridged account of Jaredites
    from 24 gold plates .... Ether 1:5; 3:17; Moroni 1:1
16. Commanded of Lord to hide Jaredite records, with
    interpreters, in earth .... Ether 4:3-5
17. Wrote the very things seen by brother of Jared .... Ether 4:4
18. Addressed future translator (Joseph Smith) concerning
    witnesses; sealed portion of plates .... Ether 5:1-4
19. To be seen at judgment seat of God at last day .... Ether 5:6; 12:38
20. Wrote concerning wickedness of secret combinations, oaths . Ether 8:20-26
21. Wrote of Ether's prophecies and teachings on faith .... Ether 12:6-41
22. Talked with Jesus face-to-face .... Ether 12:39
23. Awkward and weak in writing .... Ether 12:24, 25, 40
24. Wrote book of Moroni after abridging Jaredite record .... Moroni 1:1-4
25. Would not deny Christ, even to save life .... Moroni 1:3
26. Wrote concerning bestowal of Holy Ghost .... Moroni 2:1-3
27. Wrote concerning ordination of priests and teachers .... Moroni 3:1-4
28. Wrote concerning administration of sacramental bread ...... Moroni 4:1-3
29. Wrote concerning administration of sacramental wine .... Moroni 5:1-2
30. Wrote concerning baptism and conducting church meetings .. Moroni 6:1-9
31. Recorded words of Mormon about faith, hope, charity .... Moroni 7:1-48
32. Recorded epistle of Mormon about little children
    and baptism .... Moroni 8:1-30
33. Recorded epistle of Mormon about atrocities
    of Lamanites and Nephites .... Moroni 9:1-26
34. Wrote concerning spiritual gifts .... Moroni 10:8-17
35. Exhorted readers to pray and seek revelation of Holy Ghost .. Moroni 10:4-5
36. Bade farewell to reader until meet at judgment
    bar of the great Jehovah .... Moroni 10:34

MORONIHAH—about B.C. 50

1. Son of Moroni, the military leader .... Alma 62:43
2. Given command of Nephite armies when father retired .... Alma 62:43
3. Sent Lehi to battle with army of Coriantumr .... Helaman 1:28-29
4. With Lehi led army which slew Coriantumr,
    defeated Lamanites .... Helaman 1:30-32
5. Freed city of Zarahemla from Lamanite bondage .... Helaman 1:33
6. Established peace between Lamanites and Nephites .... Helaman 1:33

7. Army of, driven out of Zarahemla; beaten
   back to Bountiful .... Helaman 4:5-6
8. Regained many cities which had been lost to Lamanites ... Helaman 4:9-10
9. Preached righteousness to wicked Nephites .... Helaman 4:14
10. For two years led armies to new victories against Lamanites .. Helaman 4:16
11. Able to maintain lands, but unable at this time to recapture
    lost ones because of superiority of Lamanite forces .... Helaman 4:19

MORONIHAH—about A.D. 385
1. Nephite military leader of 10,000 men at Cumorah .... Mormon 6:14
2. Slain in battle .... Mormon 6:14

MOSES, Hebrew prophet
1. Divided Red Sea .... 1 Nephi 4:2; 17:26; Helaman 8:11
2. Smote rock, obtained water for Israel .... 1 Nephi 17:29
3. Delivered Israel out of Egypt .... 2 Nephi 3:10
4. Given power with a rod .... 2 Nephi 3:17
5. Given judgment in writing .... 2 Nephi 3:17
6. Not mighty in speaking .... 2 Nephi 3:17
7. To be given spokesman .... 2 Nephi 3:17
8. Face shone while in mount .... Mosiah 13:5
9. Prophesied of coming of Messiah .... Mosiah 13:33
10. Spoke of the Son of God .... Alma 33:19
11. Buried by hand of Lord .... Alma 45:19
12. Lord took him unto himself .... Alma 45:19
13. Lifted brazen serpent as type of Son of God .... Helaman 8:14
14. Death of, compared to Alma .... Alma 45:18-19

MOSIAH—about B.C. 278-130
1. Commanded by Lord to flee out of land Nephi .... Omni 12
2. Led by Lord to land Zarahemla .... Omni 13
3. Possessed brass plates of Laban .... Omni 14
4. Unable to understand language of people of Zarahemla .... Omni 17
5. Taught his language to people of Zarahemla .... Omni 18
6. Appointed as king over union of his people
   and those of Zarahemla .... Omni 19
7. Interpreted engravings on stone concerning
   people who came from Tower of Babel .... Omni 20-22
8. Died in days of Amaleki .... Omni 23
9. Succeeded by son Benjamin .... Omni 23

MOSIAH—about B.C. 154-91
1. Son of King Benjamin .... Mosiah 1:2
2. Made king over people of Zarahemla by his father .... Mosiah 1:10-15
3. Given records, sword of Laban, director, by his father .... Mosiah 1:16
4. Appointed king by command of Lord .... Mosiah 2:30
5. Kept Lord's commandments .... Mosiah 6:6
6. Labored with hands; tilled soil .... Mosiah 6:7
7. Sent 16 men to journey to land of Lehi-Nephi .... Mosiah 7:2
8. Had a "where-with" to translate languages .... Mosiah 8:13-14
9. A Seer .... Mosiah 8:13-14
10. Had gift of God to translate languages .... Mosiah 21:28

41

11. Read to his people the records of Zeniff and
    records of Alma .... Mosiah 25:1-7
12. Translated gold plates found by people
    of Limhi. (See Ether 4:1) .... Mosiah 28:11
13. Had two stones set in bow for translating .... Mosiah 28:13-16
14. Gave record and interpreters to Alma .... Mosiah 28:20
15. Recommended judge-type government instead of kings ... Mosiah 29:10-37
16. Died at age 63; reigned 33 years .... Mosiah 29:46
17. Last king of people of Nephi .... Mosiah 29:41; Alma 1:1
18. Esteemed more than any other man by his people .... Mosiah 29:40
19. Warred a good warfare in life .... Alma 1:1

MULEK—B.C. 589
1. Son of Zedekiah .... Helaman 6:10
2. Brought by Lord from Jerusalem to land north (America) ..... Helaman 6:10
3. Only son of Zedekiah not slain at time of Babylonian
   captivity (compare Jeremiah 52:10) .... Helaman 8:21
4. Progenitor of some of the people of Zarahemla .... Mosiah 25:2

MULOKI—about B.C. 100
1. Traveled with Aaron; preached in city Ani-Anti .... Alma 21:11
2. Departed and traveled to land Middoni with Aaron .... Alma 21:12
3. Cast into prison with Aaron at Middoni .... Alma 21:13; 20:2
4. Released from prison by efforts
   of Ammon, Lamoni .... Alma 20:28-30; 21:14

NEHOR—about B.C. 90
1. Man large and strong .... Alma 1:2
2. Taught false doctrine that all mankind to be saved .... Alma 1:3-5
3. Established own church .... Alma 1:6
4. Slew Gideon with the sword .... Alma 1:9; 6:7
5. Brought before Alma for judgment .... Alma 1:2-10
6. Condemned to die .... Alma 1:14
7. Confessed that he had taught untruth .... Alma 1:15
8. Guilty of priestcraft, murder .... Alma 1:11
9. Suffered death atop Hill Manti .... Alma 1:15

NEPHI—about B.C. 600
1. Son of Lehi .... 1 Nephi 2:5
2. Made record in language of father .... 1 Nephi 1:2
3. Made only partial account of father's life .... 1 Nephi 1:16-17
4. Large in stature .... 1 Nephi 2:16
5. Made an account of own life .... 1 Nephi 1:17
6. Believed in words of his father .... 1 Nephi 2:16
7. Promised by Lord he would be ruler over his brethren ..... 1 Nephi 2:19-24
8. Returned to Jerusalem with brothers to obtain brass plates .. 1 Nephi 3:9-10
9. Exhorted his brothers to be strong in faithfulness to duty ..... 1 Nephi 4:1-4
10. Slew Laban and obtained brass plates .... 1 Nephi 4:5-25
11. Persuaded Zoram to accompany him into wilderness ...... 1 Nephi 4:30-38
12. Fulness of intent was to persuade men to come to Jesus .... 1 Nephi 6:4
13. Returned with brethren to Jerusalem again .... 1 Nephi 7:3
14. Helped persuade Ishmael and family to join Lehi's group ..... 1 Nephi 7:4-5

42

15. Rebuked Laman and Lemuel for their unbelief .... 1 Nephi 7:8-15
16. Bound with cords by his brethren who seek his life .... 1 Nephi 7:16
17. Loosed from bonds by power of God .... 1 Nephi 7:17-18
18. Returned to tent of father in wilderness .... 1 Nephi 7:22
19. Made two sets of plates: one was for wars and history;
    one for ministry and things of God .. 1 Nephi 9:1-6; 19:2-5; 2 Nephi 5:29-33
20. Listened to father declare gospel; relate visions .... 1 Nephi 10:17
21. Desired to see and know things father had seen .... 1 Nephi 10:17
22. Caught away by Spirit; saw things father had seen .... 1 Nephi 11:1
23. Given interpretation of visions by an angel .... 1 Nephi 11:14
24. Had vision of birth, ministry, death of Son of God .... 1 Nephi 11:15-33
25. Saw ministry of John the Baptist .... 1 Nephi 11:27
26. Saw doings of the Lord in land of promise .... 1 Nephi 12:1-23
27. Saw mission of John the Revelator; saw John himself ..... 1 Nephi 14:18-27
28. Forbidden to write remainder of things seen in vision ..... 1 Nephi 14:28-30
29. Explained Lehi's teachings to his brethren .... 1 Nephi 15:8-36
30. Married one of Ishmael's daughters .... 1 Nephi 16:7
31. Broke steel bow; obtained no food several days .... 1 Nephi 16:18
32. Made wooden bow, arrow; guided by Lord toward food ...... 1 Nephi 16:23
33. Commanded of the Lord to build a ship .... 1 Nephi 17:8
34. With others, ate raw meat in wilderness;
    Lord made it sweet .... 1 Nephi 17:2-12
35. Mocked by daughters of Ishmael .... 1 Nephi 16:36
36. Mocked by Laman, Lemuel .... 1 Nephi 17:17-22
37. Protected by power of God which terrorized his brethren . 1 Nephi 17:52-55
38. Completed ship according to Lord's instruction .... 1 Nephi 18:2
39. Sailed with others toward land of promise .... 1 Nephi 18:8
40. Became fearful of brothers' attitude while crossing waters ... 1 Nephi 18:10
41. Cautioned brethren to remember Lord and his mercies ...... 1 Nephi 18:10
42. Bound with cords by Laman and Lemuel .... 1 Nephi 18:11
43. Loosed by them when they repent due
    to fear of great storm .... 1 Nephi 18:15-21
44. Prayed to Lord; calms great storm at sea .... 1 Nephi 18:21
45. Arrived with others in promised land .... 1 Nephi 18:23
46. Made plates of ore at Lord's command .... 1 Nephi 19:1
47. Engraved record of Lehi; account of journey in
    wilderness; Lehi's prophecies; own prophecies .... 1 Nephi 19:1
48. Quoted numerous prophets (notably Zenos) to
    persuade brethren to believe in Jesus Christ .... 1 Nephi 19:6-18
49. Read Isaiah to people to persuade them
    to believe in Redeemer .... 1 Nephi 19:23
50. Likened all scripture to his people for learning; profit ..... 1 Nephi 19:23-24
51. Quoted Isaiah, chapters 48, 49 .... 1 Nephi 20-21
52. Explained to brethren that Isaiah spoke of things both
    spiritual and temporal .... 1 Nephi 22:2-3
53. Explained future happenings upon the earth .... 1 Nephi 22:3-28
54. Testified that things written upon the brass plates are true .... 1 Nephi 22:30
55. Declared that Lehi and himself were not only
    ones who have taught these things .... 1 Nephi 22:31
56. Declared that prophecies of Joseph in
    Egypt among greatest known .... 2 Nephi 4:1-2
57. Psalm of Nephi; shortly after death of father .... 2 Nephi 4:16-35

58. Attempt made on life, by Laman, Lemuel .... 2 Nephi 5:2-4
59. Warned of Lord to flee into wilderness .... 2 Nephi 5:5
60. Took all with him who would believe in
    revelations of Lord .... 2 Nephi 5:6-7
61. Established land and people of Nephi .... 2 Nephi 5:8-9
62. Built temple, somewhat after manner of Solomon's .... 2 Nephi 5:16
63. Taught people to be industrious .... 2 Nephi 5:17
64. Consecrated Jacob, Joseph, to be priests and teachers ...... 2 Nephi 5:26
65. Declared that Isaiah, brother Jacob, and
    himself, all have seen Jesus .... 2 Nephi 11:2-3
66. Quoted much from Isaiah .... 2 Nephi 6, 7, 8
67. Quoted Isaiah .... 2 Nephi 12-24
68. Prophesied concerning Jews, Nephites
    Gentiles, Book of Mormon .... 2 Nephi 25-32
69. Not mighty in writing as in speaking .... 2 Nephi 33:1
70. Gloried in plainness and in truth .... 2 Nephi 33:6
71. Declared that he would meet mankind face-to-face
    at judgment bar of Christ .... 2 Nephi 33:10-11
72. Instructed Jacob concerning keeping of records .... Jacob 1:1-4
73. Anointed a man to be king over the people .... Jacob 1:9-11
74. Had wielded sword of Laban in defense of people .... Jacob 1:10
75. Labored all his days for welfare of people .... Jacob 1:10
76. Died, approximately 75 years old .... Jacob 1:12
77. A doer of good works .... Helaman 5:6

NEPHI—about B.C. 45
1. Eldest son of Helaman the chief judge .... Helaman 3:21
2. Succeeded his father in judgment seat .... Helaman 3:37
3. Served with justice and equity .... Helaman 3:37
4. Preached, prophesied many things to wicked Nephites ...... Helaman 4:14
5. Yielded judgment seat to Cezoram to allow
   more time for the ministry .... Helaman 5:1-4
6. Preached word of God all remainder of days .... Helaman 5:4
7. Remembered words of father about responsibility of
   following in footsteps of namesake: Nephi .... Helaman 5:6-7
8. Went from city to city teaching word of God .... Helaman 5:14-16
9. Taught with power, authority, revelation .... Helaman 5:17-18
10. With Lehi, taught among
    Lamanites; converted 8000 .... Helaman 5:18-19; Ether 12:14
11. Cast into prison by Lamanites (same prison into which
    Ammon had been cast) .... Helaman 5:21
12. Many days without food .... Helaman 5:22
13. Circled about by fire from heaven;
    protected from Lamanites .... Helaman 5:28-29
14. Preserved with Lehi by cloud of darkness;
    voice from heaven .... Helaman 5:28-34
15. Voice declared he and Lehi were servants of God .... Helaman 5:28-34
16. Face shone as angel's; appeared to converse
    with heavenly beings .... Helaman 5:35-39
17. Ministered to by angels .... Helaman 5:38-48
18. Went to land northward to preach .... Helaman 6:6
19. After six years returned to Zarahemla from north .... Helaman 7:1

44

20. Lamented over wickedness of Nephites; Gadianton Robbers . Helaman 7:2-9
21. Got upon tower to pray .... Helaman 7:10
22. Preached repentance to Nephites from the tower .... Helaman 7:11-29
23. Announced the murder of the chief judge (Seezoram) .... Helaman 8:27
24. Said brother of Seezoram was murderer (Seantum) .... Helaman 8:27
25. Accused of being in league
    with the murderer Seantum .... Helaman 9:16, 17, 23, 24
26. Arrested, bound, accused of the murder of Seezoram .... Helaman 9:19
27. Was offered bribe to confess crime of murder .... Helaman 9:20
28. Suggested a method by which real
    murderer might be found .... Helaman 9:26-36
29. Believed by some to be a prophet .... Helaman 9:40
30. Believed by some to be a god; because
    he can tell of thoughts and things .... Helaman 9:41
31. Given promise of great power, by the Lord .... Helaman 10:1-5
32. Given power to seal; loose, on earth and in heaven .... Helaman 10:6-9
33. At Lord's request, threatens people with
    destruction if not repent .... Helaman 10:11-14
34. Attacked by mob violence .... Helaman 10:15
35. Conveyed by the Spirit away from the mob .... Helaman 10:16
36. Went from place to place, teaching the people .... Helaman 10:17
37. Prayed to Lord for famine to cause people to repent .... Helaman 11:4
38. When famine had desired effect, prayed it be removed ... Helaman 11:10-18
39. People highly esteemed him as a prophet .... Helaman 11:18
40. Had many revelations daily; did much preaching .... Helaman 11:23
41. Sought out by converts of Samuel the
    Lamanite, desiring to be baptized .... Helaman 16:1-3
42. Preached, prophesied, baptized, worked miracles .... Helaman 16:4-5
43. Departed out of Zarahemla; never heard
    of again (translated?) .... 3 Nephi 1:3; 2:9
44. Had given records and sacred things to eldest son Nephi ...... 3 Nephi 1:2

NEPHI—about A.D. 1-50
 1. Eldest son of Nephi, who was son of Helaman .... 3 Nephi 1:2
 2. Given charge of sacred records and things .... 3 Nephi 1:2
 3. Kept record after departure of father .... 3 Nephi 1:2
 4. Sorrowed over wickedness of Nephites .... 3 Nephi 1:10
 5. Prayed all day on behalf of those who had faith and
    whose lives were endangered for believing in Christ .... 3 Nephi 1:11
 6. Received voice of Lord on night before Savior's birth ...... 3 Nephi 1:12-13
 7. Went forth baptizing and preaching .... 3 Nephi 1:23
 8. Visited daily by angels .... 3 Nephi 7:15-18
 9. Heard voice of the Lord .... 3 Nephi 7:15
10. Eyewitness of divine things .... 3 Nephi 7:15
11. Had revelations concerning ministry of Christ .... 3 Nephi 7:15
12. Eyewitness to quick departure of Nephites
    from righteousness to wickedness .... 3 Nephi 7:15
13. Boldly testified of repentance; remission
    of sins through Jesus Christ .... 3 Nephi 7:16
14. Had such strong words it was not possible
    for people to disbelieve him .... 3 Nephi 7:18
15. Incurred the anger of many .... 3 Nephi 7:18

45

16. Cast out devils and unclean spirits .... 3 Nephi 7:19
17. Raised brother Timothy from the dead (3 Nephi 19:4) .... 3 Nephi 7:19
18. Did many miracles in name of Jesus .... 3 Nephi 7:20; 8:1
19. Ordained men to ministry; to baptize .... 3 Nephi 7:25
20. A just man; cleansed from all iniquity .... 3 Nephi 8:1
21. At invitation, came from multitude and kissed feet of Jesus ... 3 Nephi 11:19
22. Given power from Jesus to baptize. (See note
    after material on JESUS CHRIST) .... 3 Nephi 11:21
23. One of Twelve Disciples chosen by Jesus .... 3 Nephi 19:4
24. With others of the disciples, divided multitude
    into twelve groups to teach, pray with them .... 3 Nephi 19:4-6
25. Was baptized (see note on number 22, above) .... 3 Nephi 19:11
26. Baptized the other disciples .... 3 Nephi 19:12
27. Received Holy Ghost and fire (with other disciples) .... 3 Nephi 19:11-13
28. Received ministry of angels .... 3 Nephi 19:14-15
29. Was ministered unto by Jesus .... 3 Nephi 19:15

NEPHI—about A.D. 36-110
1. Kept the record of the Nephites upon the plates of Nephi .... 4 Nephi 19
2. Died, and was succeeded in record keeping by his son Amos ... 4 Nephi 19
   Note: It appears that this man was the son of that Nephi who was one of the
   Twelve Disciples chosen by Jesus. If so, he would be the great-grandson of
   Helaman. This is concluded from the "Heading to 3 Nephi"; the "Heading to
   4 Nephi"; 4 Nephi 14, 18, and 19.

NEPHIHAH—before B.C. 67
1. Second chief judge, succeeding Alma .... Alma 4-16-18, 20
2. Elder of the church in Zarahemla; wise man .... Alma 4:16
3. Filled judgment seat with perfect uprightness before God ...... Alma 50:37
4. Had refused Alma to take possession of sacred
   records and things .... Alma 50:38
5. Died about B.C. 67 after reign of 15 years .... Alma 50:37-40
6. Was succeeded as chief judge by son Pahoran .... Alma 50:39-40

NEUM—before B.C. 600
1. Testified of crucifixion of Christ .... 1 Nephi 19:10
2. Writings of, were upon plates of brass (probably). Only once is Neum mentioned. If his writings were upon the brass plates, he must have been an Is-
   raelitish prophet living before B.C. 600, perhaps somewhere around
   Jerusalem.

NIMRAH—early Jaredite
1. Son of Akish the king .... Ether 9:8
2. Angered with Akish because Akish had slain his
   (Nimrah's) brother (name not given) .... Ether 9:8
3. Gathered a number of men and dwelt with Omner the
   deposed but rightful king .... Ether 9:9

NIMROD—before Tower of Babel—see Genesis 10:8-9
1. Mighty hunter .... Ether 2:1
2. Valley of, visited by Jared and his people .... Ether 2:1, 4

NOAH—early Jaredite
1. Son of Corihor .... Ether 7:14
2. Rebelled against King Shule (his uncle) and
   against Corihor, his father .... Ether 7:15
3. Obtained part of the kingdom for himself .... Ether 7:16
4. Captured and imprisoned King Shule—with intent to kill him .. Ether 7:17-18
5. Slain by sons of Shule who crept into Noah's
   house by night and freed Shule from prison .... Ether 7:18

NOAH—about B.C. 170-125
1. Son of Zeniff .... Mosiah 11:1
2. Became king of Nephites in land of Lehi-Nephi .... Mosiah 11:1
3. Wicked man; wine bibber, harlots,
   wealth; heavy taxes .... Mosiah 11:2-15
4. Desired to slay Abinadi, the prophet .... Mosiah 11:27-28
5. Cast Abinadi into prison .... Mosiah 12:17
6. Ordered death of Abinadi; declared him mad .... Mosiah 13:1
7. Ordered his priests (3rd time) to slay Abinadi .... Mosiah 17:1
8. Ordered the death of Alma for befriending Abinadi .... Mosiah 17:3
9. Condemned Abinadi to die unless he would retract
   his comments about Noah and his people .... Mosiah 17:7-8
10. Condemned Abinadi on grounds he said God himself
    would come to earth among men .... Mosiah 17:8
11. Delivered Abinadi to death by burning .... Mosiah 17:12
12. Fled into wilderness before Lamanite armies .... Mosiah 19:9
13. Sought by his enemy, Gideon, who nearly slew him
    at time Lamanites came .... Mosiah 19:18; 19:4
14. Suffered death by fire at hands of own
    people; fulfilling words of Abinadi .... Mosiah 19:20
15. Was succeeded by son Limhi .... Mosiah 19:26, 16, 17

OMER—early Jaredite
1. Son of King Shule .... Ether 8:1
2. Succeeded Shule as king .... Ether 8:1
3. Father of Jared .... Ether 8:1
4. Captured by his son Jared .... Ether 8:3
5. Begat Esrom and Coriantumr while in captivity .... Ether 8:4
6. Restored to kingdom through efforts of sons Esrom, Coriantumr ... Ether 8:6
7. Was plotted against by daughter of Jared, Jared,
   and Akish, who made an attempt on his life .... Ether 8:7; 9:1
8. Lost his kingdom (but not his life) to Jared, Akish .... Ether 9:1-3
9. Warned of God in a dream to depart from land; escape .... Ether 9:3
10. Restored again to throne through rebellion in
    the family of the usurper, King Akish .... Ether 9:7-13
11. Began to be old .... Ether 9:14
12. Begat Emer in his old age .... Ether 9:14; 1:29
13. Anointed Emer, who succeeded him as king .... Ether 9:14
14. Lived two years more, and died in peace, an old man .... Ether 9:15
15. Saw much sorrow in his days; much captivity, war, bloodshed ... Ether 9:15

OMNER—about B.C. 100
1. Unbeliever; son of Mosiah .... Mosiah 27:8, 34

2. Converted by angel that visited Alma, Mosiah's sons .... Mosiah 27:32
3. Preached gospel in Zarahemla .... Mosiah 27:32-37
4. Desired a mission to the Lamanites .... Mosiah 28:1-9
5. Met Alma as he (Omner) was returning with his
   brethren from 14 years preaching to Lamanites .... Alma 17:1-4
6. Desired (with Ammon) to take Anti-Nephi-Lehis to
   Zarahemla to live with Nephites .... Alma 27:4-5
7. Traveled with brethren and Ammon to investigate
   situation among Nephites, regarding the Anti-Nephi-Lehis ... Alma 27:15-16
8. Visited in Alma's home in Zarahemla .... Alma 27:20

OMNI—about B.C. 360-317
1. Son of Jarom .... Omni 1
2. Commanded by Jarom to keep record; preserve genealogy .... Omni 1
3. Fought with sword to defend Nephites from Lamanites .... Omni 2
4. Declared himself to be wicked man, not keeping
   commandments as ought to have done .... Omni 2
5. Gave plates to son Amaron after brief mention of
   wars and times of peace among the Nephites .... Omni 3

ORIHAH—early Jaredite
1. Son of Jared .... Ether 6:14
2. Appointed king over Jaredite people .... Ether 6:27
3. Walked humbly before the Lord; people prospered .... Ether 6:28-30
4. Lived exceeding many days; a righteous king .... Ether 7:1
5. Begat 23 sons; 8 daughters .... Ether 7:2
6. Was succeeded as king by son Kib .... Ether 7:3

PAANCHI—about B.C. 50
1. Son of Pahoran (I), the chief judge .... Helaman 1:3
2. Rebelled violently against the people and against
   his brother Pahoran (II) over the judgment seat .... Helaman 1:7
3. Drew a following away after him in the rebellion .... Helaman 1:7-9
4. Was tried and condemned to death, according
   to the law, for his rebellion .... Helaman 1:8

PACHUS—about B.C. 60
1. King of dissenters from Nephite government;
   Kingman; against Pahoran (I) .... Alma 62:8
2. Slain in Zarahemla battle against combined
   forces of Moroni, Pahoran (I) .... Alma 62:8

PACUMENI—about B.C. 45
1. Son of Pahoran (I) the chief judge .... Helaman 1:3
2. Struggled for judgment seat; yielded to Pahoran (II),
   his brother, because of voice of the people .... Helaman 1:6
3. Appointed chief judge after brother,
   Pahoran (II), was murdered .... Helaman 1:13
4. Pursued and slain by Coriantumr, Lamanite general .... Helaman 1:21

PAGAG—early Jaredite
1. Eldest son of brother of Jared .... Ether 6:25

48

2. Selected by people to be king; declined the honor . . . . Ether 6:25

PAHORAN (I)—about B.C. 67-52
1. Son of Nephihah . . . . Alma 50:39-40
2. Third chief judge and governor of the Nephites . . . . . . Alma 50:39-40; 61:1-2
3. Took oath, ordinance, to judge righteously;
   maintain religious freedom; keep the peace . . . . Alma 50:39
4. Became chief judge about B.C. 67 . . . . Alma 50:40
5. Refused to alter the law to change
   government from a republic to a kingdom . . . . Alma 51:2-3
6. Retained his office against dissenters by a popular vote . . . . Alma 51:4-7
7. Received epistle from Moroni, concerning need of
   supplies, men, at the battlefront . . . . Alma 59:1-13
8. Received second epistle from Moroni; was sorely
   chastened for his supposed indolence and neglect . . . . Alma 60:1-36
9. Wrote epistle to Moroni, protesting his innocence
   but declaring a rebellion in the government at home . . . . Alma 61:1-21
10. Joined forces with Moroni to drive out dissenters (Pachus) . . . . Alma 62:6-7
11. Restored to the judgment seat; dissenters slain; imprisoned . . . . . Alma 62:8
12. With Moroni and large body of men, marched to land
    Nephihah with intent to overthrow Lamanites in that city . . . . Alma 62:14
13. Slew many Lamanites . . . . Alma 62:15
14. Caused many Lamanites to take oath of peace toward Nephites . Alma 62:16
15. Sent 4,000 oath-taking Lamanites to dwell
    with people of Ammon . . . . Alma 62:17
16. With Moroni, captured Lamanite city Nephihah
    without loss of one Nephite; many Lamanites slain . . . . Alma 62:26
17. Returned from battlefield to judgment seat . . . . Alma 62:44
18. Died, after sixteen-year reign as chief judge . . . . Alma 50:40; Helaman 1:1, 2
19. Father of Pahoran, Paanchi, Pacumeni, many other sons . . . . Helaman 1:3-4

PAHORAN (II)—about B.C. 45
1. Son of Pahoran (I), the chief judge . . . . Helaman 1:3
2. Appointed to judgment seat after death of father . . . . Helaman 1:4-5
3. Had contended with his brethren Paanchi,
   Pacumeni, over the judgment seat . . . . Helaman 1:2-3
4. Murdered by Kishkumen while upon judgment seat . . . . Helaman 1:9

RIPLAKISH—middle Jaredite
1. Son of King Shez . . . . Ether 10:4; 1:24
2. King of Jaredites after death of father . . . . Ether 10:4
3. Wicked king; concubines, taxes, prisons . . . . Ether 10:5
4. Built many spacious buildings with tax money . . . . Ether 10:5
5. Erected exceedingly beautiful throne . . . . Ether 10:6
6. Built many prisons into which he put all who
   would not pay heavy taxes . . . . Ether 10:6
7. Worked prisoners or put them to death . . . . Ether 10:6
8. Caused prisoners to work fine workmanship; gold, etc. . . . . Ether 10:7
9. After reign of 42 years, people rebelled . . . . Ether 10:8
10. Slain in the rebellion; descendants driven away . . . . Ether 10:8
11. Had descendant named Morianton who regained kingdom . . . . . . Ether 10:9

49

SAM—about B.C. 600

SAMUEL—about B.C. 6

SARIAH—about B.C. 600

5. Entered ship with family to sail to promised land .... 1 Nephi 18:8
6. Much grieved because of wickedness of Laman, Lemuel .. 1 Nephi 18:17-18
7. Mother of at least six sons, two daughters ... 1 Nephi 2:5; 18:7; 2 Nephi 5:6

SATAN
1. Enticed Adam, Eve to eat forbidden fruit .... Helaman 6:26-29
2. Plotted with Cain for murder of Abel .... Helaman 6:26-29
3. Inspired building of Tower of Babel .... Helaman 6:26-29
4. Inspired and misled the Jaredites .... Helaman 6:26-29
5. Inspired Gadianton to plot, murder by secret oaths .... Helaman 6:26-29
6. Author of all sins .... Helaman 6:30
7. Handed down plots, oaths, from generation to generation .... Helaman 6:30

SEANTUM—about B.C. 20
1. Brother of Seezoram, the chief judge .... Helaman 8:27; 9:26
2. Murdered Seezoram in garb of secrecy .... Helaman 9:26
3. When accused of the murder, at first denied;
   became nervous and confessed .... Helaman 9:26-38

SEEZORAM—about B.C. 20
1. Chief judge .... Helaman 8:27; 9:23, 26
2. Murdered in secrecy by his own brother, Seantum ... Helaman 8:27; 9:6, 26
3. There was mourning, fasting, burial for .... Helaman 9:10

SHARED—late Jaredite
1. Defeated, captured King Coriantumr .... Ether 13:23
2. Vanquished by sons of Coriantumr, who returned
   the kingdom to their father .... Ether 13:24
3. Alternately conquered, then was beaten by Coriantumr ..... Ether 13:27-30
4. Slain by Coriantumr, after having inflicted a
   severe wound in Coriantumr's thigh .... Ether 13:31

SHEREM—about B.C. 540
1. Anti-Christ; sought opportunity to talk with Jacob .... Jacob 7:1-4
2. Confounded by Jacob .... Jacob 7:8-12
3. Demanded a sign by Holy Ghost; stricken .... Jacob 7:13-15
4. Feared eternal punishment, hell; confessed sin, died .... Jacob 7:16-20

SETH—late Jaredite
1. Son of Shiblom .... Ether 11:9; 1:11
2. Brought into captivity all his days .... Ether 11:9
3. Begat son Ahah, who reigned over kingdom all
   his days, which were few .... Ether 11:10; 1:10

SHEM—about A.D. 385
1. Nephite military leader with 10,000 men at Cumorah .... Mormon 6:14
2. Slain in battle .... Mormon 6:14

SHEMNON—about A.D. 33
1. One of Twelve Disciples chosen by Jesus .... 3 Nephi 19:4
2. Present on occasion with others .... 3 Nephi 12:1; 28:1-3

51

SHEZ—middle Jaredite
1. Descendant (son?) of Heth .... Ether 10:1; 1:25
2. Began to build up a broken and fallen people .... Ether 10:1
3. Remembered wickedness and destruction of fathers,
   and established a righteous kingdom .... Ether 10:2
4. Eldest son, Shez, rebelled against him .... Ether 10:3
5. Builder of cities .... Ether 10:4
6. Lived to exceeding old age and begat Riplakish .... Ether 10:4
7. Died, and was succeeded by son Riplakish .... Ether 10:4

SHEZ—middle Jaredite
1. Eldest son of King Shez .... Ether 10:3
2. Rebelled against his father .... Ether 10:3
3. Exceeding rich; smitten by a robber .... Ether 10:3

SHIBLOM—late Jaredite
1. Son of Com .... Ether 11:4; 1:12
2. Slain in battle .... Ether 11:9
3. Begat son named Seth (note different spelling of
   Shiblon in this verse. Compare Ether 1:11) .... Ether 11:9
4. Put prophets to death .... Ether 11:5
5. Great calamities and famines in his day .... Ether 11:6-8

SHIBLOM—about A.D. 385
1. Nephite military leader with 10,000 at Cumorah .... Mormon 6:14
2. Slain in battle .... Mormon 6:14

SHIBLON—about B.C. 74-53
1. Son of Alma .... Alma 31:6-7
2. Accompanied Alma, others to preach to
   apostate Zoramites .... Alma 31:6-7
3. Blessed; commanded by his father .... Alma 38:1
4. Blessed by father, Alma .... Alma 45:15
5. Ordained to Holy Order of God; preached
   gospel; had been baptized .... Alma 49:30
6. Succeeded Helaman as head of church .... Alma 63:1
7. Given sacred records and things .... Alma 63:1
8. Just man, kept commandments .... Alma 63:2
9. Was brother of Helaman .... Alma 63:2
10. Died after conferring sacred things upon nephew
    Helaman, son of Helaman (B.C. 53) .... Alma 63:1-11

SHIZ—late Jaredite
1. Vanquished Coriantumr's army .... Ether 14:16
2. Brother of Lib .... Ether 14:17
3. Slew men, women, children; burned cities .... Ether 14:17
4. Swore to avenge death of brother Lib .... Ether 14:24
5. Severely wounded Coriantumr .... Ether 14:30
6. Received epistle from Coriantumr asking for end of war .... Ether 15:4-5
7. Asked for privilege of personally slaying
   Coriantumr with own sword .... Ether 15:5
8. Continued the war .... Ether 15:5-27

9. Swore to slay Coriantumr or die himself .... Ether 15:28
10. After six days battle, fainted from loss of blood .... Ether 15:20-29
11. Beheaded by Coriantumr .... Ether 15:30
12. Raised on hands, struggled for breath, and died .... Ether 15:31

SHULE—middle Jaredite
1. Son of Kib's old age .... Ether 7:7; 1:31
2. Born while father was in captivity to Corihor .... Ether 7:7
3. Mighty in strength and judgment .... Ether 7:8
4. Angered with brother Corihor .... Ether 7:8
5. Made swords of steel for his followers .... Ether 7:9
6. Overthrew Corihor, gave kingdom back to their father, Kib .... Ether 7:9
7. Peacefully succeeded his father as king .... Ether 7:10
8. A righteous king over a numerous people .... Ether 7:11
9. Begat many sons and daughters .... Ether 7:12
10. Gave Corihor power in the kingdom .... Ether 7:13
11. Was rebelled against by nephew Noah, son of
    brother Corihor .... Ether 7:14-16
12. Captured, imprisoned by Noah .... Ether 7:17
13. Rescued by his sons at night, when about to be slain by Noah ... Ether 7:18
14. Restored to his kingdom .... Ether 7:18
15. Slew Corihor, son of Noah .... Ether 7:21
16. Gave power and favor to Nimrod, son of Shule .... Ether 7:22
17. Protected prophets of God from revilings of the people .... Ether 7:24-25
18. Begat sons and daughters in old age .... Ether 7:26
19. A righteous king .... Ether 7:27
20. Father of Omer, who succeeded him as king .... Ether 8:1

TEANCUM—about B.C. 67
1. Appointed by Moroni to head off Morianton's rebellion .... Alma 50:35
2. Slew Morianton near narrow neck of land
    called Desolation .... Alma 50:34-35; 51:29
3. Brought prisoners back and placed them in their own land .. Alma 50:35-36
4. Fought with Amalickiah's forces in land Bountiful .... Alma 51:29
5. Slew Amalickiah with javelin to heart while he slept in tent ... Alma 51:33-34
6. Stood ready next day to battle Lamanites .... Alma 52:1
7. Prepared his army for great battle against Lamanites now
    led by Amalickiah's brother, Ammoron .... Alma 52:5-7
8. Held council of war with Moroni in land Bountiful .... Alma 52:19
9. Helped regain city Mulek by strategy and decoy .... Alma 52:21-26
10. Wished well by Pahoran in letter to Moroni .... Alma 61:21
11. With Lehi, placed in command of army at battlefront while
    Moroni took task force to aid Pahoran because of rebellion
    at seat of government .... Alma 62:3
12. Later joined forces with Moroni, Pahoran, in land
    Moroni, in pursuit of Lamanite army; camped for the night ... Alma 62:32-35
13. Angered with Ammoron, whom he considered the
    cause of the present war .... Alma 62:35
14. Slipped into Ammoron's tent at night; cast javelin
    near his heart; died, but not until roused guards .... Alma 62:36
15. Slain by Ammoron's servant .... Alma 62:36
16. True friend of liberty; had suffered many afflictions .... Alma 62:37

TEOMNER—about B.C. 63
1. Nephite soldier stationed by Helaman with small band—
   for strategem—in wilderness near city Manti (see Gid) ...... Alma 58:16-17
2. Destroyed Lamanite spies and guards at city Manti .... Alma 58:20-21
3. Took city Manti from Lamanites because of cleverness of Helaman
   in placing of armies to lure Lamanites out of city .... Alma 58:21-22

TIMOTHY—about A.D. 33
1. Brother of Nephi .... 3 Nephi 19:4
2. One of Twelve Disciples chosen by Jesus .... 3 Nephi 19:4
3. Raised from the dead by Nephi .... 3 Nephi 19:4; 7:19
4. Present on occasion with others .... 3 Nephi 12:1; 28:3

TUBALOTH—about B.C. 50
1. King of Lamanites .... Helaman 1:16
2. Son of Ammoron .... Helaman 1:16
3. Appointed Coriantumr leader over Lamanite armies .... Helaman 1:17

TWELVE DISCIPLES (sometimes referred to as Special
Disciples)—about A.D. 33
1. Chosen by Jesus; given power to baptize .... 3 Nephi 12:1; 11:18-41
2. Given special instructions by Jesus .... 3 Nephi 13:25-34
3. Served as ministers to multitude for
   sacramental emblems .... 3 Nephi 18:1-10
4. Given power to confer Holy Ghost .... 3 Nephi 18:36-37
5. Name of each one given .... 3 Nephi 19:4
6. Each taught segment of multitude .... 3 Nephi 19:5-6
7. Prayed for reception of Holy Ghost .... 3 Nephi 19:9
8. Were baptized and received Holy Ghost
   (see note, Jesus Christ, No. 20) .... 3 Nephi 19:10-13
9. Received ministry of angels .... 3 Nephi 19:14-15
10. Prayed to Jesus as their Lord and God .... 3 Nephi 19:17-18
11. Shone with whiteness while praying .... 3 Nephi 19:25-30
12. Again administered sacramental emblems to multitude ...... 3 Nephi 20:1-7
13. Taught, baptized as many people as would come .... 3 Nephi 26:17
14. United in fasting and mighty prayer .... 3 Nephi 27:1
15. Wondered as to proper name of the church .... 3 Nephi 27:3
16. Jesus appeared to, and explained proper name of church .. 3 Nephi 27:4-11
17. To be judges of the Nephites .... 3 Nephi 27:27; Mormon 3:19
18. Each one given desire: 9 desired to speedily enter Lord's
    kingdom at end of life; 3 desired to remain in ministry
    until Jesus' second coming. Each to receive desire .... 3 Nephi 28:1-11
19. See Three Nephites, in Appendix I
20. Went to paradise of God, except three who should tarry .... 4 Nephi 14
21. To be judged by the Twelve at Jerusalem .... Mormon 3:19

ZARAHEMLA—about B.C. 122
1. Descendant of Mulek .... Mosiah 25:2; Omni 15
2. Rejoiced exceedingly because Lord sent people of Mosiah
   with plates of brass, record of the Jews .... Omni 14
3. Gave a genealogy of his fathers, according to memory .... Omni 18

ZEDEKIAH—about B.C. 600
1. King of Judah (see Jeremiah 52:1) .... 1 Nephi 1:4; Omni 15
2. Carried away captive into Babylon .... Omni 15
3. Suffered loss of all sons except Mulek .... Helaman 8:21
4. Seed of, with Nephites .... Helaman 8:21

ZEDEKIAH—about A.D. 33
1. One of Twelve Disciples chosen by Jesus .... 3 Nephi 19:4
2. Present with others on occasion .... 3 Nephi 12:1; 28:3
3. See also Twelve Disciples

ZEEZROM—about B.C. 82
1. Lawyer in city Ammonihah; very expert .... Alma 10:30-32
2. Questioned Amulek, with trickery .... Alma 11:21-45
3. Confounded by Amulek; trembled with fear .... Alma 11:46
4. Asked questions about resurrection and judgment .... Alma 12:8
5. Repented; defended Alma, Amulek before the people .... Alma 14:6-7
6. Cast out by the people .... Alma 14:6-7
7. Seized by severe fever; thought that his wickedness
   had caused death of Alma, Amulek .... Alma 15:3
8. Healed and baptized by Alma; began preaching .... Alma 15:5-12
9. Went with Alma to preach to Zoramites .... Alma 31:6-7
10. Evidently preached among the Lamanites also .... Helaman 5:40-41
11. Apparently returned to Zarahemla with Alma, others .... Alma 35:14

ZEMNARIHAH—about A.D. 20
1. Appointed leader of Gadianton band,
   succeeding Giddianhi .... 3 Nephi 4:17
2. Led robbers in seige against Nephites .... 3 Nephi 4:17
3. Failed to conquer; withdrew armies to land northward .... 3 Nephi 4:23
4. Cut off in retreat; captured by armies of Gidgiddoni .... 3 Nephi 4:24-27
5. Hanged until dead upon top of tree; then tree was felled ...... 3 Nephi 4:28

ZENEPHI—about 385 A.D.
1. Nephite general in last struggle; took provisions
   from needy women and children of Nephites .... Moroni 9:16

ZENIFF—about B.C. 200-160
1. Taught in all language of the Nephites .... Mosiah 9:1
2. Left land of Zarahemla with expedition to find
   land of Lehi-Nephi .... Mosiah 7:13; 8:2; 7:9; Omni 28
3. Sent as spy to observe Lamanite forces before destroying them . Mosiah 9:1
4. Desired not to destroy Lamanites; rather make treaty .... Mosiah 9:1-2
5. Contended with ruler of expedition to make treaty .... Mosiah 9:2
6. Was ordered slain by the ruler .... Mosiah 9:2
7. Rescued from death after much war and bloodshed .... Mosiah 9:2
8. Returned to Zarahemla with scant
   50 survivors of expedition .... Mosiah 9:2; Omni 8
9. Collected another expedition to find land Lehi-Nephi .... Mosiah 9:3
10. Overzealous to inherit land of fathers .... Mosiah 9:3; 7:21
11. Made treaty with King Laman, concerning
    possession of land .... Mosiah 9:5-7; 7:21

12. Became king over his people in land Nephi .... Mosiah 7:21
13. Was deceived by Laman's lies, craftiness .... Mosiah 10:18
14. Fought with own hands, even in old age,
    against Lamanites .... Mosiah 9:14; 10:21
15. With own hands helped bury the dead .... Mosiah 9:19
16. Conferred kingdom upon son Noah .... Mosiah 11:1
17. A good man .... Mosiah 10:19; 11:1, 2

ZENOCK—before B.C. 600
1. Predicted wicked men would crucify Christ .... 1 Nephi 19:10
2. Testified that mercy comes because of Son of God .... Alma 33:15-16
3. Of the tribe of Joseph .... 3 Nephi 10:16
4. Testified many things concerning Christ .... Alma 34:7; 33:15-17
5. Writings of, upon plates of brass .... 1 Nephi 19:21; 3 Nephi 10:16-17
6. Stoned to death; martyr for truth .... Alma 33:17

ZENOS—before B.C. 600
1. Testified of Christ being buried in sepulchre; 3 days
   of darkness .... 1 Nephi 19:10
2. Testified of thunderings, lightnings, tempest, fire,
   smoke, mountains moving, etc., at crucifixion of Christ ...... 1 Nephi 19:11
3. Testified of rending of rock .... 1 Nephi 19:12
4. Spoke of persecution of Jews; gathering of Israel .... 1 Nephi 19:13-16
5. Gave lengthy parable of scattering, gathering of Israel .... Jacob 5:1
6. Gave instructions concerning prayer .... Alma 33:3
7. Said redemption came through Son of God .... Alma 34:7
8. Slain for his prophecies .... Helaman 8:19
9. Spoke of restoration of Lamanites to the gospel .... Helaman 15:11
10. Of tribe of Joseph .... 3 Nephi 10:16
11. Writings of, on plates of brass .... 3 Nephi 10:17; 1 Nephi 19:21

ZERAHEMNAH—about B.C. 74
1. Lamanite leader in war against Nephties .... Alma 43:5
2. Chose Zoramites, Amalekites as chief captains over
   Lamanite forces because they were most wicked .... Alma 43:6
3. Desired power and authority .... Alma 43:8
4. Led Lamanite army, armed with swords, cimeters, bows,
   arrows, stones, slings; naked except girdle about loins .... Alma 43:20
5. Feared to battle Moroni's forces, because equipped
   with shields, head plates, arm-shields, breastplates, etc. .... Alma 43:19-22
6. Was surrounded by strategy of Moroni .... Alma 43:51-53
7. Rejected offer of peace from Moroni; said
   Lamanites would perish or conquer .... Alma 44:8-9
8. While in peace conference, attempted to slay Moroni .... Alma 44:12
9. Scalped by soldier of Moroni; returned to own camp .... Alma 44:12
10. When saw how Nephites defeated Lamanites, surrendered
    and promised never war any more .... Alma 44:19

ZERAM—about B.C. 87
1. One of four spies sent by Alma to watch Amlicites .... Alma 2:21-22
2. Returned with word that Amlicites and Lamanites coming .... Alma 2:23-26
3. See Amnor, Manti, Limher

ZORAM—B.C. 600
1. Servant of Laban, followed Nephi outside Jerusalem walls . 1 Nephi 4:20-35
2. Held firm in arms of Nephi; could not escape .... 1 Nephi 4:31
3. Persuaded by Nephi to join Lehi's party ...... 1 Nephi 4:33-34; Alma 54:23
4. Made oath to follow Nephi and party henceforth .... 1 Nephi 4:35-38
5. Married eldest daughter of Ishmael .... 1 Nephi 16:7
6. Entered ship to sail for promised land .... 1 Nephi 18:8
7. Was blessed by Lehi .... 2 Nephi 1:30-32
8. Journeyed with Nephi into wilderness away from Laman .... 2 Nephi 5:6
9. True friend of Nephi forever .... 2 Nephi 1:30

ZORAM—about B.C. 80
1. Chief captain over Nephite armies .... Alma 16:5
2. Had two sons; Lehi, Aha .... Alma 16:5
3. Desired to deliver captured brethren from Lamanites .... Alma 16:5-6
4. Crossed river Sidon; with sons defeated Lamanites;
   returned the captured brethren .... Alma 16:7-8

ZORAM—about B.C. 74
1. Leader of Zoramites (apostate Nephites) to whom Alma
   preached .... Alma 30:59
2. Led his people to worship dumb idols .... Alma 31:1
3. Demanded people of Ammon not receive Zoramite
   converts; was not obeyed .... Alma 35:8

PART 2
UNNAMED PERSONS

*An Analytical Biography of persons somewhat significant
to the Book of Mormon story, but unnamed in the record,*

AMALEKITE CONTENDER WITH AARON—between B.C. 90-77
1. Citizen of city of Jerusalem .... Alma 21:4
2. Contended verbally with Aaron in the synagogue .... Alma 21:5
3. Expressed severe doubt, criticism, concerning gospel .... Alma 21:5-8
4. Believed that God would save all men .... Alma 21:6
5. Did not believe in Son of God .... Alma 21:7-8
6. Disbelieved Aaron's testimony concerning Jesus Christ ...... Alma 21:9-10

ATTEMPTED SLAYER OF AMMON—about B.C. 90
1. Brother of a man slain by Ammon .... Alma 19:22
2. Attempted to slay Ammon with sword while Ammon was
   overcome by the Spirit of the Lord .... Alma 19:22
3. Fell dead in the attempt .... Alma 19:22-24

BROTHER OF AMALEKI—about B.C. 130
1. Went with Zeniff on second expedition from
   Zarahemla with intent to find land Nephi .... Omni 29-30; Mosiah 9:3

BROTHER OF JARED—early Jaredite
*Although unnamed in the record itself, the Prophet Joseph stated that his
name was Mahonri Moriancumr. The Improvement Era, 8:705. Burton,
Discourses of the Prophet Joseph Smith, p. 206.*
1. Came with Jared and families from great tower .... Ether 1:33
2. Large and mighty man—highly favored of the Lord .... Ether 1:34
3. At Jared's request, prayed that language of self and
   friends not be confounded .... Ether 1:34-37
4. At Jared's request, prayed to know of destination .... Ether 1:38-39
5. Commanded by Lord to gather possessions, flocks, travel
   to choicest land of the earth .... Ether 1:40-43; 2:1
6. Traveled with family and friends to valley of Nimrod .... Ether 2:1, 4
7. Gathered fowls, fish, honey bees, and seeds .... Ether 2:2-3
8. Was given instructions for travel from Lord in cloud .... Ether 2:4-5
9. Built barges to cross many waters .... Ether 2:6
10. Approached the great sea which divided the lands .... Ether 2:13
11. After four years, visited again by Lord in cloud .... Ether 2:14
12. Chastened for three hours because had not prayed diligently .... Ether 2:14

58

13. Obtained aid of people in building barges as per
    Lord's instructions (8 barges) .... Ether 2:16; 3:1
14. Made holes for air—per Lord's instructions .... Ether 2:19-24
15. Procured 16 small transparent stones for light in barges .... Ether 3:1
16. Prayed to Lord about fallen nature of man .... Ether 3:2
17. Pleaded with Lord that He touch stones with finger, to shine ...... Ether 3:4
18. Saw Lord's finger and was struck with fear .... Ether 3:6, 19; 12:20-21
19. Commended by Lord for great faith .... Ether 3:9
20. Saw and talked with spirit body of Jesus Christ .... Ether 3:10-17, 20
21. Was instructed to hide knowledge of vision from the world
    until after Christ came in the flesh .... Ether 3:21; 4:1
22. Was instructed to write the vision in unknown language .. Ether 3:22, 27;4:1
23. Received 2 stones for interpretation, to be sealed up
    with the writings (compare D&C 17:1) .... Ether 3:23, 24, 28
24. In vision, beheld all earth's total inhabitants .... Ether 3:25
25. Saw things as great as any man ever saw .... Ether 4:4
26. Placed the stones in the vessels .... Ether 6:2
27. Boarded vessels and put forth upon the sea .... Ether 6:4-8
28. Sang praises of thankfulness to Lord .... Ether 6:9
29. Sailed 344 days .... Ether 6:11
30. Tilled the soil and thanked the Lord .... Ether 6:13
31. Had 22 sons and daughters .... Ether 6:15, 20
32. Began to be old .... Ether 6:19
33. Refused to constrain eldest son (Pagag) to become king,
    although the people urged him .... Ether 6:25
34. Died .... Ether 6:29
35. By faith had removed mountain Zerin .... Ether 12:30
36. Beheld all things by faith .... Ether 12:21
37. Mighty in writing—even to overpowering them who read .... Ether 12:24

BROTHER OF KIM—middle Jaredite
1. Rebelled against and overthrew his brother, King Kim .... Ether 10:14
2. Kept Kim in captivity all remainder of Kim's days .... Ether 10:14

BROTHER OF SHIBLOM—late Jaredite
1. Rebelled against Shiblom, the king; started great war .... Ether 11:4
2. Put many of the prophets of the Lord to death .... Ether 11:5

DAUGHTER OF ISHMAEL—about B.C. 600
1. With her mother, defended Nephi in opposition to Laman,
   Lemuel, and two of her own brothers .... 1 Nephi 7:19
2. Probably the girl who later married Nephi .... 1 Nephi 16:7

DAUGHTER OF JARED—early Jaredite
1. Daughter of Jared who was son of Omer, the king .... Ether 8:8
2. Exceeding expert (in wickedness) .... Ether 8:8
3. Saw sorrow of father when he lost the kingdom .... Ether 8:8
4. Devised plan whereby to reclaim kingdom for father .... Ether 8:8
5. Exceeding fair .... Ether 8:9
6. Reminded father of plan of ancients to get gain, glory;
   as written in the ancient records .... Ether 8:9,17

7. Proposed to dance before Akish to lure him into
   killing King Omer, her own grandfather .... Ether 8:10
8. Danced before and pleased Akish who desired her to wife .... Ether 8:11
9. Married Akish .... Ether 9:4

DAUGHTERS OF THE LAMANITES—between B.C. 145-123
1. Gathered at place in Shemlon to sing, dance, make merry ..... Mosiah 20:1
2. Only small number gathered one certain day .... Mosiah 20:2
3. Twenty-four were kidnapped by priests of King Noah .... Mosiah 20:5
4. Later pled with own people not to slay the priests,
   who were now their husbands .... Mosiah 23:30-34

DAUGHTERS OF LEHI—about B.C. 600
1. At least two in number .... 2 Nephi 5:6
2. Believed in revelations, visions .... 2 Nephi 5:6
3. Went with Nephi; away from Laman, Lemuel .... 2 Nephi 5:6

FIVE MEN—about B.C. 23
1. Investigated murder of chief judge, as prophecied
   by Nephi .... Helaman 9:1
2. At first did not believe Nephi's prophecy .... Helaman 9:2
3. Found judge to be dead; Nephi's prophecy to be true .... Helaman 9:3
4. Fell to earth with astonishment .... Helaman 9:4-5
5. Were accused of the murder; placed in prison .... Helaman 9:7-9
6. Brought before group of judges; rehearsed their story .... Helaman 9:10-16
7. Testified to truth of Nephi's words .... Helaman 9:15, 18
8. Were liberated on day of chief judge's burial .... Helaman 9:18
9. Were liberated because of confession of Seeantum
   (murderer) .... Helaman 9:38
10. Had converted some while in the prison .... Helaman 9:39

FREEMEN—about B.C. 67-62
1. Desired that Pahoran (I) should retain judgment seat .... Alma 51:6
2. Covenanted to maintain free government .... Alma 51:6
3. Contended with king-men, who wanted kingdom instead
   of republic with judges .... Alma 51:4-7
4. Gained the victory by popular vote .... Alma 51:7
5. Supported Pahoran again, 5 years later, against other
   dissenters similar to king-men .... Alma 62:3-17
6. Joined with Moroni's task force in conquering rebels .... Alma 62:1-6

GADIANTON ROBBERS—from about B.C. 50 to A.D. 385
1. Caused almost entire overthrow of Nephites .... Helaman 2:13-14
2. Built up among Lamanites .... Helaman 11:24-33
3. Dwelt upon the mountains .... 3 Nephi 1:27
4. Increased in numbers .... 3 Nephi 1:28-30
5. Wrought much havoc .... 3 Nephi 2:11
6. Were resisted by many who were righteous, both
   Nephites and Lamanites .... 3 Nephi 2:12-18
7. Many were placed in prison; there taught the word of God ...... 3 Nephi 5:4
8. Temporarily out of operation .... 3 Nephi 5:6
9. Revived again in few years .... 3 Nephi 6:28-29

10. Destroyed in destruction at death of Jesus Christ ... 3 Nephi 8:1; 9:9; 10:12
11. Revived again in 3rd century A.D., among Nephites .... 4 Nephi 42-46
12. Infested the Lamanites .... Mormon 1:18
13. Mormon fought against, in closing battles of Nephites ..... Mormon 2:27-28

HIGH PRIEST OF KING GILEAD—late Jaredite
1. Murdered Gilead, brother of Shared, as he sat upon throne ...... Ether 14:9
2. Was secretly murdered by Lib, a man of
   secret combination .... Ether 14:10

KING OF LAMANITES—between B.C. 145-123
1. Led his armies against people of Limhi, supposing
   them to be the kidnappers of 24 Lamanite daughters .... Mosiah 20:6-7
2. Was left on battlefield among dead, although
   only wounded .... Mosiah 20:12
3. Taken before King Limhi for questioning .... Mosiah 20:13-14
4. Accused people of Limhi of carrying away Lamanite girls ..... Mosiah 20:15
5. Was pacified toward Limhi's people when learned that
   Noah's priests were real kidnappers .... Mosiah 20:24
6. Proposed to Limhi that they go unarmed before Lamanite
   armies; promised no harm would come .... Mosiah 20:24
7. Pled with Lamanite armies on behalf of Limhi and people .. Mosiah 20:25-26
8. Returned in peace with his people to own land .... Mosiah 20:26

KING OF LAMANITES—about B.C. 90
1. King of all Lamanites .... Alma 20:8
2. Angry at son Lamoni for not attending the feast .... Alma 20:9
3. Accused Nephi, son of Lehi, of having been a liar,
   robber; says Ammon is also .... Alma 20:10-13
4. Commanded Lamoni to slay Ammon with sword .... Alma 20:14
5. Attempted to slay son, Lamoni, for refusing to slay Ammon ..... Alma 20:16
6. Attempted to slay Ammon himself .... Alma 20:20
7. Physically overpowered by Ammon; pleads for life;
   grants Ammon his desires, even to half of kingdom .... Alma 20:23
8. Granted Lamoni freedom in the kingdom .... Alma 20:24-27
9. Granted Ammon's brethren release from prison; favors ..... Alma 20:24-27
10. Visited by Aaron (Ammon's brother); was taught
    repentance .... Alma 22:1-18
11. Sank to earth, overcome with Spirit of God .... Alma 22:18
12. Repented of sins; converted whole household to the Lord ...... Alma 22:23
13. Commanded protection to all servants of the Lord .... Alma 23:1
14. Conferred kingdom on son, Anti-Nephi-Lehi; died B.C. 80 ..... Alma 24:3-4

KING OF LAMANITES—about B.C. 72
1. Stirred up by Amalickiah to anger against Nephites .... Alma 47:1
2. Sent proclamation for people to gather, fight Nephites .... Alma 47:1
3. Was rebuffed by majority of his people who desired not
   to fight Nephites, but nevertheless were afraid of king .... Alma 47:2
4. Was wroth because of disobedience of his people .... Alma 47:3
5. Placed Amalickiah in command of that portion
   that would fight .... Alma 47:3
6. Gave Amalickiah authority to compel people to fight .... Alma 47:3

7. Was betrayed by Amalickiah whom he trusted .... Alma 47:4-16
8. Lived in city Nephi; land Nephi .... Alma 47:20
9. Came out of city to meet Amalickiah, supposing him to have
   fulfilled his request to compel men to arms .... Alma 47:21
10. Received servants of Amalickiah in token of peace .... Alma 47:22-23
11. Was stabbed to death by servant of Amalickiah .... Alma 47:24
12. Was succeeded in the kingdom by Amalickiah who also
    married his wife, the queen .... Alma 47:35

KING-MEN—about B.C. 67
1. Men of high birth, power, among Nephites .... Alma 51:8
2. Desired chief judge Pahoran (I) to alter law to change
   government from judges to king .... Alma 51:2-4
3. Were rebuffed by Pahoran .... Alma 51:3
4. Sought to depose Pahoran .... Alma 51:4-5
5. Contended with the freemen, who favored Pahoran and
   free government .... Alma 51:4, 7
6. Lost to freemen in popular vote .... Alma 51:7
7. Refused to take arms in defense of country against Lamanites .. Alma 51:13
8. Were marched against by armies of Moroni who desired to
   compel them to fight for protection of country .... Alma 51:14-18
9. Four thousand slain by Moroni's armies .... Alma 51:19
10. Many imprisoned by Moroni; trials postponed because of
    urgency of the war (see No. 13) .... Alma 51:19
11. Some king-men became defenders of country .... Alma 51:20
12. Put to an end by Moroni; no more called king-men .... Alma 51:21
13. Those imprisoned (No. 10) received trials six years later .... Alma 62:9
14. Many executed according to law for traitorous acts in time
    of war .... Alma 62:9
15. Given choice of fight for country, or be put to death .... Alma 62:9

LAMANITE GUARDS AT CITY GID—about B.C. 63
1. Received Laman (a Nephite sympathizer) as a friend .... Alma 55:8
2. Desired to drink wine which Laman brought .... Alma 55:9-10
3. Freely consumed wine and became drunken .... Alma 55:11-18
4. Fell into deep sleep .... Alma 55:15-16
5. Were surrounded by Moroni's armies in the nighttime .... Alma 55:21
6. Threw down weapons; pled for mercy at feet of Moroni's men ... Alma 55:23
7. Were made prisoners of Moroni's army .... Alma 55:25
8. Made to labor to fortify city Gid for Nephites .... Alma 55:25
9. Were transferred as prisoners to city Bountiful .... Alma 55:26
10. Tried many intrigues to escape; not successful .... Alma 55:27-32
11. Attempted to poison Nephites with wine; not successful ..... Alma 55:30-32

LEADER OF ZARAHEMLA SCOUTING EXPEDITION—about B.C. 130
1. Strong and mighty man; stiffnecked .... Omni 28
2. Led group of men from Zarahemla in search of land Nephi ..... Omni 27-28
3. Caused a contention among the expedition .... Omni 28
4. Austere, bloodthirsty man .... Mosiah 9:2
5. Ordered Zeniff slain .... Mosiah 9:2

MEN OF LIMHI—LAND NEPHI SCOUTING EXPEDITION—about B.C. 122
1. Forty-three men sent by King Limhi from land Nephi
   in search of land Zarahemla .... Mosiah 8:7; 21:25
2. Purpose was to appeal to people of Zarahemla to deliver
   Limhi's people from Lamanite bondage .... Mosiah 8:7
3. Became lost in wilderness .... Mosiah 8:8; 21:25
4. Found land covered with bones of men, beasts;
   supposed it to be land Zarahemla;
   also found many waters .... Mosiah 8:8; 21:26
5. Found ruins of buildings; weapons of war; very large .... Mosiah 8:8, 11
6. Returned to land Nephi with record on 24 gold plates
   they found with the bones; also brought
   some weapons .... Mosiah 8:8-11; 21:26-27; Ether 1:1-2; 15:33

MIGHTY MAN—late Jaredite
1. Member of secret combination .... Ether 11:15
2. Wrested one-half of Jaredite kingdom from Moron .... Ether 11:15
3. Maintained one-half of kingdom for many years .... Ether 11:15
4. Was overthrown by Moron and lost kingdom to him .... Ether 11:16

MIGHTY MAN—late Jaredite
1. Descendant of brother of Jared .... Ether 11:17
2. Overthrew Moron, and obtained the kingdom .... Ether 11:18
3. Kept Moron in captivity the remainder of his (Moron's) days .... Ether 11:18

MORIANTON'S MAID SERVANT—about B.C. 67
1. Was beaten by Morianton in his anger .... Alma 50:30
2. Told Moroni of Morianton's plan for rebellion .... Alma 50:31

QUEEN OF LAMANITES—between B.C. 90-77
1. Wife of Lamoni's father (probably Lamoni's mother) .... Alma 22:1, 19
2. Was informed by king's servants that king
   had fallen as though dead .... Alma 22:19
3. Was angry with Aaron whom she supposed had slain
   her husband the king .... Alma 22:19
4. Commanded servants to slay Aaron and companions .... Alma 22:19
5. Was disobeyed by fearful servants .... Alma 22:20-21
6. Was filled with fear lest she too be smitten .... Alma 21:21
7. Commanded servants to gather enough people to slay
   Aaron and his brethren .... Alma 22:21
8. Saw Aaron raise the king from the earth—alive .... Alma 22:22-23
9. Was converted unto the Lord .... Alma 22:23; 23:3

QUEEN OF LAMANITES, wife of Lamoni—about B.C. 90
1. Mourned two days and nights over Lamoni whom she
   thought dead .... Alma 18:43
2. Sent for Ammon; requested he see Lamoni, whom some
   say is dead and stinketh .... Alma 19:2-5
3. Had some doubt as to whether Lamoni really dead .... Alma 19:5
4. Was informed by Ammon that Lamoni not dead; not to be buried . Alma 19:8
5. Was informed by Ammon that King Lamoni would rise
   on morrow .... Alma 19:8

6. Believed on words of Ammon .... Alma 19:9
7. Was told by Ammon that she had greater faith than any
   Nephites .... Alma 19:10
8. Watched over bed of husband, Lamoni, until morrow .... Alma 19:11
9. Addressed by husband when he rose .... Alma 19:12
10. With husband was overcome with Spirit; both sank to earth .. Alma 19:13-18
11. Raised by Abish, one of her women servants .... Alma 19:16-29
12. Praised Jesus when she arose .... Alma 19:29
13. Possibly spoke in tongues .... Alma 19:30
14. Raised her husband from the ground .... Alma 19:30

QUEEN OF LAMANITES, wife of Amalickiah—about B.C. 72
1. Wife of Lamanite king in city and land of Nephi .... Alma 47:32
2. Was informed by embassy from Amalickiah that husband
   had been slain .... Alma 47:32
3. Requested Amalickiah come in person, with witnesses,
   to discuss death of the king .... Alma 47:33
4. Was falsely informed that husband had been slain
   by own servant .... Alma 47:34
5. Gave favor to Amalickiah; married him .... Alma 47:35

ROBBER—middle Jaredite
1. Smote, probably killed, Shez, the son of Shez,
   because of his great riches .... Ether 10:3

SECOND KING OF NEPHITES—about B.C. 540
1. Appointed by Nephi to be king after him .... Jacob 1:9-11
2. Given name-title of second Nephi .... Jacob 1:11

SERVANT OF AMMORON—about B.C. 61
1. Awakened by Ammoron's groanings; slew Teancum .... Alma 62:36

SERVANT OF HELAMAN—about B.C. 50
1. Through disguise, obtained knowledge of secret plan to
   slay Helaman the chief judge .... Helaman 2:6
2. Met Kishkumen, gave him a sign, learned of murderous
   plot to kill Helaman .... Helaman 2:7
3. Was requested by Kishkumen to lead him to judgment seat .... Helaman 2:7
4. Pretended to lead Kishkumen toward Helaman's
   judgment seat .... Helaman 2:8
5. Stabbed Kishkumen in the heart, that he died without groan ... Helaman 2:9
6. Ran and told Helaman all that he had seen, heard, done ..... Helaman 2:10

SERVANTS OF KING OF LAMANITES—about B.C. 73-63
1. Falsely accused by Amalickiah's servants of killing king ..... Alma 47:25-26
2. Were sought by army, which thought they were the killers ...... Alma 47:28
3. Departed out of land Nephi; joined people
   of Ammon in land Zarahemla .... Alma 47:29
4. One, named Laman, aided Moroni in recapture of city Gid .... Alma 55:4-16

SOLDIER OF MORONI—about B.C. 74
1. Protected Moroni, and scalped Zerahemnah the Lamanite
leader as Zerahemnah rushed in to slay Moroni .... Alma 44:12
2. Held scalp on sword point, high in air; threatened Lamanites
with similar fate .... Alma 44:13-14

SON OF AKISH—middle Jaredite
1. Was shut up in prison and starved to death
through jealousy of father (King Akish) .... Ether 9:7
2. Brother of Nimrah, who avenged his death .... Ether 9:8-13

SON OF CEZORAM—about B.C. 25
1. Appointed to judgment seat vacated by murder of his father .. Helaman 6:15
2. Murdered the same year by one of Gadianton's band .... Helaman 6:15

SONS OF AKISH—middle Jaredite
1. Had sworn to support wickedness of their father,
but broke their oath for own selfish aims .... Ether 9:10-11
2. Led many people away from following Akish, by offering them
money of their own; appealed to greedy persons .... Ether 9:10-11
3. Rebelled in open war against their father .... Ether 9:12
4. Caused almost complete destruction of kingdom of Akish .... Ether 9:12

THREE NEPHITE DISCIPLES—around A.D. 33
1. Were likened unto John the Beloved .... 3 Nephi 28:1-6
2. Were given power over death until time of Jesus'
2nd coming; were to behold all doings of
the Father among men .... 3 Nephi 28:7; Ether 12:17
3. Neither to taste nor endure pains of death .... 3 Nephi 28:8
4. Not to have physical pain .... 3 Nephi 28:9, 38
5. Not exempt from sorrow for sins of world .... 3 Nephi 28:9, 38
6. Desired to bring souls unto Christ as long as
the earth should stand .... 3 Nephi 28:9
7. To have fulness of joy; sit down in Father's kingdom .... 3 Nephi 28:10
8. To become even as Christ .... 3 Nephi 28:10
9. Caught up to heaven; saw and heard unspeakable things . 3 Nephi 28:13, 36
10. Had not power to utter what glorious things saw, heard ...... 3 Nephi 28:14
11. Seemed to be transfigured .... 3 Nephi 28:15
12. Ministered unto men on earth; baptizing, etc., ... 3 Nephi 28:16-18
13. Cast into prison by enemies; could not be held ... 3 Nephi 28:19; 4 Nephi 30
14. Cast into pits by enemies; could not be held .... 3 Nephi 28:20
15. Thrice cast into furnace; no harm (4 Nephi 33) .... 3 Nephi 28:21
16. Twice cast into den of wild beasts; no harm (4 Nephi 33) ...... 3 Nephi 28:22
17. Preached gospel of Christ to all people of Nephi .... 3 Nephi 28:23
18. Names of, not given to the world .... 3 Nephi 28:25
19. Ministered to Mormon, Moroni (Mormon 8:11) .... 3 Nephi 28:26
20. To be among the Gentiles, but unknown by them .... 3 Nephi 28:27
21. To be among Jews, but unknown by them .... 3 Nephi 28:28
22. To minister to all scattered tribes of Israel .... 3 Nephi 28:29
23. To minister to all nations, kindreds, tongues, people .... 3 Nephi 28:29
24. Are as angels of God; show selves to whom please .... 3 Nephi 28:30

25. Great, marvelous works to be wrought by them .... 3 Nephi 28:31-32
26. Received partial bodily change, but not equal to
    change coming upon their bodies at last day .... 3 Nephi 28:36-40
27. Remained on earth after other nine had died .... 4 Nephi 14
28. Wrought mighty miracles among the people .... 4 Nephi 30
29. Were true believers; true worshippers of Christ .... 4 Nephi 37
30. Sorrowed for sins of world .... 4 Nephi 44
31. By A.D. 300 were almost only righteous among Nephites .... 4 Nephi 46
32. Were withdrawn from Nephites sometime after A.D. 310 .... 4 Nephi 48

TWENTY-FOUR NEPHITES —about A.D. 385
1. Survived the terrible battle at Cumorah .... Mormon 6:11, 15
2. Were probably slain later by Lamanites .... Mormon 8:2-3, 7

TWO THOUSAND YOUNG MEN OF AMMON AND HELAMAN—
about B.C. 65
1. Were anxious to fight in defense of country .... Alma 53:16-18
2. Wanted Helaman to be their leader .... Alma 53:19
3. Were honest, faithful, trustworthy .... Alma 53:20-21
4. Were descendants of Laman, son of Lehi .... Alma 56:3
5. Went forth to defend their country .... Alma 56:5
6. Were children of converted Lamanites .... Alma 56:3-6
7. Marched with Helaman to city of Judea .... Alma 56:9-10
8. Joined army of Antipus .... Alma 56:30-36
9. Decoyed most powerful Lamanite army into
   the wilderness from city Antiparah .... Alma 56:30-36
10. Led by Helaman; showed supreme courage in battle .... Alma 56:45-48
11. Were all very young men .... Alma 56:46
12. Were known as sons of Helaman .... Alma 56:46
13. Trusted in God, and the teachings of their mothers .... Alma 56:46-48
14. Not one was slain in battle with Lamanites .... Alma 56:55-56
15. Joined by an additional 60 of their brethren .... Alma 57:6
16. Fought valiantly against Lamanites; remarkably
    preserved from death, although 200 received wounds ...... Alma 57:19-25
17. Were preserved by their strong faith in God .... Alma 57:26-27
18. Not one soul fell in battle; although many wounded .... Alma 58:39-40
19. Very careful to observe commandments of Lord, daily .... Alma 58:40

WIFE OF ISHMAEL—about B.C. 600
1. Defended Nephi, with her daughter, against Laman,
   Lemuel, and two of her sons .... 1 Nephi 7:19

Appendix I

A Description of the Plates of the Book of Mormon

Members of The Church of Jesus Christ of Latter-day Saints accept without reservation the fact that on the twenty-second day of September, 1827, the Prophet Joseph Smith came into possession of an ancient record written upon plates "having the appearance of gold" from which, by miraculous means, he translated what is known as the Book of Mormon. This sacred record, written upon metal plates, was entrusted to the Prophet's care until the work required of him in translating was completed, at which time the record was returned to the custody of the heavenly messenger, the angel Moroni, who had delivered it to him.

This sacred, ancient record was shown only to a small number of persons. The record itself forbade the showing of it to any except a few whom the Lord would choose for the purpose of being witnesses. (2 Nephi 27:12-13; Ether 5:2-3.) The number of official witnesses who saw the plates, and who had a firsthand knowledge of their appearance, seems to be limited to twelve.[1] Few others, if any, had the privilege of seeing them.[2]

It seems to be the way of spiritual things that the majority of the people do not see with their eyes, but rather are obliged to believe on the testimony of those witnesses who have seen. The essential part of the testimony is that the plates exist and were translated. Details about size, weight, and number are of secondary importance.

Each copy of the Book of Mormon contains the "Testimony of Three Witnesses" and also the "Testimony of Eight Witnesses," which affirm plainly that the witnesses have seen the plates, but both testimonies are notably silent as to precise and detailed information concerning the number, size, and probable weight of the plates. The "Testimony of Eight Witnesses" tells of "hefting" the record, which gives an indication that they are heavy.

Thus there is scant information available about the exact size, weight, or number of the plates. Several of the witnesses commented briefly about these items but with some variation.

The Prophet Joseph Smith, the translator, chief witness, and best informed person in this dispensation in regard to the plates, shed some light on the sub-

---

[1]These are Joseph Smith, the Three Witnesses, and the Eight Witnesses.
[2]There is a report of David Whitmer's mother, Mrs. Peter Whitmer, having seen the plates. This is published in an interview of David Whitmer with Orson Pratt and Joseph F. Smith, in the *Deseret Evening News* (Salt Lake City), November 16, 1878.

ject in a letter written on March 1, 1842, to John Wentworth, editor of the Chicago *Democrat:* "These records were engraved on plates which had the appearance of gold; each plate was six inches wide and eight inches long and not quite as thick as common tin. They were filled with engravings, in Egyptian characters, and bound together in a volume as the leaves of a book with three rings running through the whole. The volume was something near six inches in thickness, a part of which was sealed. The characters on the unsealed part were small, and beautifully engraved."[3]

Although the foregoing statement contains some very descriptive information, it does not say anything about the number of plates, the weight, and how much of the record was sealed.

Information given by some of the early brethren who were associated with the Prophet is enlightening, although somewhat variable. David Whitmer, one of the Three Witnesses, said shortly before his death, while being interviewed by a representative of the Kansas City *Journal:* "They appeared to be of gold, about six by nine inches in size, about as thick as parchment, a great many in number and bound together like the leaves of a book by massive rings passing through the edges."[4]

Brother Whitmer's description makes the plates somewhat larger than the Prophet's account, but there is an agreement in substance as to appearance, thickness of each leaf, and the manner by which they were bound together. No mention is made of the weight, but a suggestion is made as to the abundance of the plates.

Martin Harris, another of the Three Witnesses, estimated the plates to be eight by seven inches, each plate being as thick as thick tin, and the volume to be four inches in thickness.[5] That Brother Harris had a personal, firsthand knowledge of the physical properties of the plates is clear, for he explained: "I know of a surety the work is true; for did I not at one time hold the plates on my knees for an hour and a half, while in conversation with Joseph, when we went to bury them in the woods that the enemy might not obtain them? . . . And as many of the plates as Joseph Smith translated, I handled with my hands, plate after plate."[6]

No mention was made by either David Whitmer or Martin Harris (two of the Three Witnesses) that a part of the plates was sealed, nor did they make any reference to the weight.

It appears that neither Oliver Cowdery, who was one of the Three Witnesses, nor any of the Eight Witnesses left a record giving the dimensions or description of the plates.

Orson Pratt, who was not an eye-witness of the plates so far as we know, but who was close to the Prophet and those who were eye-witnesses, wrote this concerning the record: "Each plate was not far from seven by eight inches in width and length, being not quite as thick as common tin. They were filled on both sides with engravings, in Egyptian characters, and bound together in a volume, as the leaves of a book, and fastened at one edge with three rings running through the whole. This volume was something near six inches in thickness, a part of which was sealed."[7]

---

[3]Joseph Smith, *History of the Church of Jesus Christ of Latter-day Saints,* 4:537.

[4]J. M. Sjodahl, *An Introduction to the Book of Mormon* (Salt Lake City: Deseret News Press, 1927), p. 38.

[5]George Reynolds, *The Myth of the Manuscript Found* (Salt Lake City: Juvenile Instructor Office, 1883), p. 89.

[6]*Ibid.,* p. 88.

[7]Orson Pratt, *Interesting Account of Several Remarkable Visions* (Edinburgh: Balantyne and Hughes, 1840), p. 13.

Sixteen years later, while speaking in the Tabernacle at Salt Lake City, Elder Pratt is reported to have said that "about two-thirds [of the plates] were sealed up."[8] He said nothing about the weight or the number of leaves.

It might be argued, with good cause, that since Elder Pratt was not given a special view of the plates, his testimony on the matter should not be equal with the others; but anyone familiar with Elder Pratt's logical and analytical manner and his thoroughness of investigation will not dismiss his statements lightly. It seems likely that he would have asked many if not all of the witnesses as to size and other detailed information before forming his conclusions.

President George Q. Cannon wrote that the plates were eight inches in width and formed a book about six inches in thickness. He said also that about one-third of the volume was sealed, but that "the other leaves Joseph turned with his hand."[9] Nothing was mentioned about length, weight, or number of plates.

The following table summarizes some of the main features of the reports given by the brethren as discussed above.

A Comparison of Various Descriptions of the Gold Plates

Name	Width	Length	Thickness of volume	Weight	Sealed part
Joseph Smith	6"	8"	6"	n/c*	part
David Whitmer	6"	9"	n/c	n/c	n/c
Martin Harris	7"	8"	4"	n/c	n/c
Orson Pratt	7"	8"	6"	n/c	2/3
Geo. Q. Cannon	8"	n/c	6"	n/c	1/3
Three Witnesses (Official Testimony)	n/c	n/c	n/c	n/c	n/c
Eight Witnesses (Official Testimony)	n/c	n/c	n/c	"hefted"	n/c

*No Comment.

Inasmuch as we are not sufficiently informed as to the number of leaves, their exact size, or their composition (whether gold or alloy), it is impossible to correctly ascertain the exact weight of the plates. Estimates have been placed from about 125 to less than 50 pounds.[10]

There is yet another facet to discuss about the description of the plates. It was mentioned previously that Elder Orson Pratt said that "about two-thirds [of the plates] were sealed up, and Joseph was commanded not to break the seal; that part of the record was hid up."[11] Elder Pratt seemed to imply a larger sealed portion than President Cannon had indicated. However, we do not know the thickness of each leaf of the sealed portion, and it is possible he might have been speaking of the number of plates, rather than of the actual measurement in inches.

---

[8]*Journal of Discourses,* 3:347.

[9]George Q. Cannon, *Life of Joseph Smith* (Salt Lake City: Juvenile Instructor Office, 1888), pp. 49-50.

[10]Sjodahl, *op cit.,* pp. 36, 43-44.

[11]*JD,* 3:347.

In the testimonies of the Three Witnesses and the Eight Witnesses there is no mention that any part was sealed. The foregoing table illustrates that the Prophet Joseph Smith, President Cannon, and Elder Pratt each said the volume was six inches in thickness. They mentioned also that a part was sealed. Brother Whitmer made no mention of the thickness of the volume, nor did he mention a sealed part, whereas Martin Harris gave the thickness of the volume to be four inches (considerably less than that given by the others) but did not mention any sealed portion. Thus, whenever a sealed portion was mentioned, the volume was consistently spoken of as being six inches. If the entire volume (sealed and unsealed) equaled six inches, and if one-third of it was sealed, then the unsealed part would equal the four inches spoken of by Martin Harris. This may account for the different descriptions. The fact that Brothers Harris and Whitmer were eye witnesses and had handled the plates might suggest that they were describing only the unsealed portion that the Prophet had translated.

Is it possible that the unsealed portion was sometimes detached from the sealed portion during the time Joseph Smith was translating? Such a procedure would make for ease in handling, since the plates were relatively heavy and would be cumbersome. While working with the translation and moving the plates, it would be a convenience to handle only the part to be translated. Since neither Brother Harris nor Brother Whitmer mention anything about a sealed portion, it may be that they were describing only the plates that were used in the translation of the Book of Mormon and which did not include the sealed portion.

That the Three Witnesses may have viewed only the unsealed portion of the plates is suggested by a number of factors: first, by their individual expressions already quoted; second, from the report that an angel came and showed them the plates and "turned over the leaves one by one," which would not be the case with sealed plates; and third, from a voice that spoke to the witnesses at the time saying: "These plates have been revealed by the power of God, and they have been translated by the power of God. The translation of them which you have seen is correct, and I command you to bear record of what you now see and hear."[12]

Since the sealed plates were not translated by Joseph Smith,[13] the voice, of necessity, was speaking of the unsealed portion. The record of these events denotes that the witnesses were seeing precisely the plates that had been translated and that were not sealed.

---

[12]*HC*, 1:54-55.
[13]See 2 Nephi 27:7-10; Ether 5:1.

Appendix II

Some Observations

1. Nephite medical practice; roots, herbs to cure fevers. (Alma 46:40.)

2. War crime trials. (Alma 51:13-19 and 62:9-10.)

3. Only three women are mentioned by name (Sariah, Isabel, and Abish), although many others figure prominently in the story.

4. There are no names in the Book of Mormon beginning with the letters D, F, Q, U, V, W, X, Y. The most common is A, with 36 personal names beginning with this letter.

5. Handwriting on the wall. (Alma 10:1-3; similar to Daniel 5.)

6. Members of the church were called "Christians" by nonmembers, and perhaps not as a compliment. (Alma 46:13-16.) This is similar to circumstances in the New Testament (Acts 11:26) in which many Bible students feel that the word *Christian* was at first applied to the believers by the unbelievers.

7. Mormon and Moroni: Mormon was a great military leader. No doubt, while he was reviewing and abridging the Nephite record, he was impressed with the doings of the great general Moroni and was moved to name his own son in honor of him. (Alma 48:11-18.)

8. The Nephites and the Jaredites probably never met, but both had dealings with the people of Mulek—at different times. (Omni 12-22.)

9. The land southward was a game preserve; the Jaredites brought animals in their barges. (Ether 2:1-3; 6:4.) They were coming to a "new" land after the flood, and one with perhaps no animals thereon. During the latter end of the Jaredite nation, the Lord sent poisonous serpents to hedge up the way and drive the Jaredite animals southward. This was a punishment to the Jaredites, but stocked the land southward with game. (Ether 9:31-32; 10:19-21.) Soon after, when Lehi's party landed in the area, they were impressed with the variety and quantity of the forest animals. (1 Nephi 18:24-25.) The

71

Nephites had not been instructed to bring animals with them, as the Jaredites had been. (1 Nephi 18:6.) That which was a cursing to the Jaredites was a blessing to the Nephites. (Compare Ether 10:20-21; 13:21; and Mormon 5:19.)

10. Lehi and Jacob as theologians and philosophers: These two prophets appear to be the two greatest philosophers among Book of Mormon writers. It is interesting that of the blessings Lehi gave to his sons, that which he gave to Jacob is the most philosophical in content. (2 Nephi 2.) The blessing fits the mind and disposition of Jacob, who is the outstanding doctrinal teacher of the Book of Mormon.

11. Fury of the Lamanite prisoners: In one instance the Lamanite prisoners were so eager to escape that while being marched to prison by Nephite guards they became extremely unruly. The Nephites fixed their swords to meet the charge. The front line of the Lamanites ran upon the swords, thus permitting the remainder of the Lamanites to escape while the Nephite swords were impaled in the Lamanite bodies. (See Alma 57:28-33.)

12. The Book of Mormon is essentially without humor, except for a few inferences: Alma 9:2-3; 57:10; 55:30-32. Omni 9 is perhaps more explicit. Chemish admits that sometimes they did not write in the record until the day it was to be handed to the next historian. We may see a similarity in this to the methods of some present-day students who do their work about the time it is due.

13. War: The Book of Mormon includes a record of much armed warfare. Many have wondered why a scriptural and spiritual book would have such a preoccupation with war. Perhaps it is to impress the reader that freedom is worth fighting for, even at the cost of lives and bloodshed. It might also be saying further that man will most likely have to fight to maintain his freedom.

14. Mormon's editorial comments: The Book of Mormon is more than a report of facts. It is an interpretation of these facts. Several times, after reporting an event or a series of events, Mormon, the editor, says, "and thus we can plainly discern that . . . " — and then he proceeds to explain the significance of the events. Examples of such helpful editorializing are found in Alma 24:30; Helaman 3:27 and 12:1.

15. Teaching by contrast: Perhaps one of the reasons why the Book of Mormon is such a converter of the hearts of men is that the message is made plain by vivid contrast. When speaking of the resurrection, for example, it is the most righteous and the most wicked who are compared. (Alma 11:44-45.) The record tells of saints and sinners in strong opposition to one another, such as Nephi and Laban (1 Nephi 17), Jacob and Sherem (Jacob 7), Alma and Korihor (Alma 30), Moroni and Amalickiah (Alma 51), and many others. The story of Alma's conversion fairly sparkles with contrasts of gloom and joy; he experiences "inexpressible horror" on the one hand, and sweet, exquisite joy on the other. (Alma 36:14, 21.) At the point of death Sherem the anti-Christ fears the consequences and speaks "of hell, and of eternity, and of eternal punishment." (Jacob 7:18.) However, two pages later Enos, the prophet, approaches death with a feeling of rejoicing, and he anticipates the day when he shall see the face of the Lord with pleasure. (Enos 26-27.)

72

Appendix III

Some Specific Categories Showing Occupations, Callings, Other Identifying Characteristics

This listing does not include every person in the text, but only the most prominent ones for whom there is significant identification. Because some persons occupied a number of positions in life, many are listed under more than one category. Page numbers have reference to the alphabetical section of this treatise.